Developed through various faculty projects at:
Orange Christian School - Orange, California
Agape Force Prep School - Lindale, Texas
and
Kingwood Academy - Kingwood, Texas

Under the Leadership of Ken Marks

Adapted and expanded by

Beverly Caruso

and

Debbie Peterson

Table of Contents

Introduction

What is character? It is the combination of attributes one has that is determined by the individual's will. As we read the Scriptures we discover God's Character. **He** is truth. **He** is just. **He** is love. **He** is life. He cannot be other than pure and holy.

What kind of Character does He want for us? For our children? Micah 6:8 poses the question and provides the answer: "What does the Lord require of you? To **act justly** and to **love mercy** and to **walk humbly** with your God."

We can learn Character and become men and women of Character only by learning God's Character and allowing His life and nature to be reflected in us – as the sun's light is reflected by the moon.

How then, is Godly Character formed - in our own lives and in our children's? In a society where Godly Character is becoming scarce, this question is on the hearts of many. How can God's Character be developed in anyone's life?

God's Word instructs us, "make every effort to add to your faith, goodness; and to goodness, knowledge; and to knowledge, self-control; and to self-control, perseverance; and to perseverance, godliness; and to godliness, brotherly kindness; and to brotherly kindness, love." 2 Peter 1:5.

Abraham Lincoln said, "Character is like a tree and reputation like a shadow. The shadow is what we think of it, the tree is the real thing."

Chuck Colson says that someone who perseveres in doing what is right develops a reliable character. And Aristotle said, "Moral excellence comes about as a result of habit. We become just, by doing just acts; brave, by doing brave acts."

In his book *Mere Christianity*, C.S. Lewis writes that becoming virtuous is like becoming an athlete. Even a bad tennis player might make a good shot now and then by sheer luck. But a truly good player, Lewis writes, is someone who has practiced making good shots for years, "whose eye and muscles and nerves have been so trained...that they can now be relied on."

We have discovered that all issues of life may be viewed through any of the Character Qualities of God. In fact, all of the Character Qualities are about life. There are overlaps on what a person, family or group is going through. When creative individuals grasp this concept, it is like having a handle on dealing with things as they arise in our lives. Studying Character Qualities provides practical ways to deal with problems.

In the past, parents could rely on the influence of the extended family and long-time family friends to model Godly Character Qualities before their children. Society as a whole – church, school, government - reinforced the Godly principles parents taught their children.

As Josh McDowell points out, today we've moved from a Judeo-Christian Society, through the Post-Judeo-Christian Society, to an Anti-Judeo-Christian Society. Those who take a stand for Godly values and morality are assaulted with accusations of intolerance, judgmentalism, and anti-multiculturalism.

Many Christian parents have given up trying to counter the ungodly influence of their children's heroes, such as rock singers and movie stars; but we have received a clear mandate from God to "train up a child in the way he should go." **He** hasn't given up on them. We, as Christian parents, tend to congratulate ourselves if we take our children to Sunday School, remove them from public school, enroll them in private, Christian schools, or even (as a growing number of parents are doing) teach their children at home. But, regardless of what setting we have designated for their academic training, we must remember: God gave us - the parents - the responsibility of training our children. We must take the initiative to see that our children develop Godly Character Qualities in their lives.

This book is designed as a guide and resource for parents to form Godly Character in their own lives and in the lives of their children. The format makes it suitable for either individual or group study for people of all ages. You may want to use all or only a portion of the material.

It is our prayer that *Developing Godly Character in Children* will assist you in your effort to prepare your children for life.

Beverly Caruso, Ken Marks, and Debbie Peterson

How to Use this Handbook

We use the term curriculum, not to imply that only parents who serve as their children's primary academic teacher may use this study, rather as a term that speaks of a planned course of study. Although presented here for use by individual families, it may also be used in Sunday school and children's church as well as in its original setting, the Christian school. Instructions are included for adaptation for these settings on page 26.

We suggest that one Major Character Quality be studied for about three months with each Sub-Quality taking about a week. In addition, two shorter Units, "Wisdom" and "Loyalty" are designed to be studied for two weeks each year. If such a plan is followed, the entire curriculum will cover three Major Character Qualities each year, or four if a Unit is covered during summer months. It will take 2-3 years before repeating a Unit.

After completing the course of study you will have...

- studied and participated in character-building Projects for eight Major Qualities: Brotherly Love, Fear of the Lord, Faith, Joy, Integrity, Responsibility, Obedience, and Virtue, plus Love - God's Grace
- memorized important portions of Scripture (of 10-20 verses each) related to each Quality studied
- learned facts about important, larger portions of Scripture or important scriptural concepts related to the Character Quality studied
- learned ten Christian hymns of the faith
- studied numerous Bible passages in view of Character Qualities modeled

Over the years we have joyously discovered many benefits in having the entire family/group studying the same Character Quality, memorizing the same Scripture Passages, and learning the same Bible Facts together. This provides a unifying focus around which parents encourage one another, pray, and brainstorm. It helps unite rather than divide the Bible study efforts of families with more than one child, making it possible for older and younger children to work together on Projects. If given the opportunity, kindergartners and junior highers gravitate to each other naturally and lovingly - as do 3-year-olds and 73-year-olds!

On the other hand, having uniform subject matter has never produced study courses that were unimaginative "look-alikes" from group to group; nor has returning periodically to the same Character Qualities produced dull repetition. God's character is too broad, His Word too deep, and most Christian parents too creative for that. *Developing Godly Character in Children* is exciting!

Overview

Developing Godly Character in Children is a unit study approach to studying Godly Character Qualities. You will choose one of eight Major Character Qualities (with their Sub-Qualities) to study for up to three months.

The Major Qualities

- Brotherly Love
- Faith
- Fear of the Lord
- Integrity
- Joy
- Obedience
- Responsibility
- Virtue

The first step is to set individual goals using the Goal Setting Chart on Page 9, and the Positive/Negative Character Qualities Lists on Pages 11-14.

After making copies of the Master Lesson Plan on the inside of the back cover, you'll plan a course of study. It is simply a matter of filling in the blanks, then following the plan. You can use as many of the individual aspects of the course as you choose. You may use all of the elements one day and only a few the next.

Each Unit Includes:

✓ A **Key Verse** for each Major and Sub-Quality
✓ A Working **Definition** for each Major and Sub-Quality
✓ **Hymns** for joyful worship
✓ **Scripture Passage** for Memorization or Meditation
✓ **Bible Facts** of important, related concepts
✓ **Scriptures** for devotional or Study purposes
✓ **Project and Activity** suggestions for practical, hands-on growth

Two shorter units, Wisdom and Loyalty, are designed for two one-week courses *each* year.

In addition, because no parent wants his child simply to develop Godly Character Qualities without coming to know the One whose love gave His Son for the forgiveness of our sins, we have included a study of Love - God's Grace, the plan of God's salvation for mankind. These Unit Studies follow the same format as the other Major Qualities.

Elements of Each Unit of Study

Key Verses

The Key Verse is memorized and discussed at the beginning of the Unit of Study. It can also provide the framework for a group Character Project.

Definitions

Two Definitions are given, where possible, for each Quality: a Working Definition, and those from the *American Dictionary of the English Language* by Noah Webster, published in 1828 by G. & C. Merriam Company, republished in 1967 by the Foundation for American Christian Education. In some cases the form or tense of the word is different from the one used here.

The Working Definitions are designed to zero in on one or more specific issue with which we often struggle in developing a given Quality (e.g., in developing Loyalty, we struggle with speaking well of others). Working Definitions produce useful starting points for Projects in individual character growth.

The Working Definitions began largely as slight modifications of those published by the Institute in Basic Life Principles (used with permission of the I.B.L.P.). They have evolved over the years as the authors encountered other sources and used them with children. Generally, Definitions have become simpler. As such, they are not only easier for children to grasp and memorize, they also seem to *hit home* more forcefully with adults.

The Definitions from the *American Dictionary of the English Language* are given primarily for purposes of comparison. Many Christians will be surprised at the changes in meaning that words have taken in two centuries. You may choose to have older children memorize some of the old Webster's Definitions.

The Definitions can be profitably used:

- by parent/classroom teachers, to inspire lessons and Projects
- by children, to help identify and express praise for positive Qualities in themselves, their siblings, classmates, and others
- by parents, to help children recognize character needs and develop individual character-building Projects
- in group settings of adults and teens as an aid in affirming one another
- in a variety of other ways which will be discovered, and their number expanded, through brainstorming sessions

4 – Developing Godly Character in Children

Why study the definitions of 180 years ago? Studying Webster's old dictionary can be a worthwhile pursuit. Noah Webster had more influence on the American English language than any other person, living or dead. He worked for forty-five years, learning twenty languages, and comparing up to thirty dictionaries from many languages, in order to clearly state the true meaning of words. Modern atheists have diluted the meaning of many English words.

It is upon this foundation that our American language and our educational system were established. Many of our founding fathers, including George Washington and Benjamin Franklin, looked to Noah Webster as an authority.

"Though long 'regulating' his 'conduct by the precepts of the Christian faith', Noah Webster resisted such teachings as regeneration, atonement, and the divinity of Christ. He describes his resistance to things spiritual by concluding, I "closed my books, yielded to the influence which could not be resisted or mistaken, and was led by a spontaneous impulse to repentance, prayer, and entire submission of myself to my Maker and Redeemer. My submission appeared to be cheerful, and was soon followed by that peace of mind which the world can neither give nor take away." From the Introduction to the republished edition of *Webster's American Dictionary of the English Language.*

The full, republished text of Noah *Webster's American Dictionary of the English Language* can be obtained from: The Foundation for American Christian Education, P.O. Box 27035, San Francisco, CA 94127.

Sub-Qualities Related to the Major Quality may be used to focus on a certain area of need within a Major Quality to expand the understanding and to provide a different approach on a second time through the Major Quality.

Hymns

We trust no justification need be offered for teaching our children to memorize and sing with enthusiasm Christian Hymns of the Faith! We highly recommend that the entire family memorize at least two verses for "heads-up," joyful worship. The musical notes of the Hymns may be found in many old hymnals:

Wisdom
Jesus Loves Even Me

Loyalty
Blest Be the Tie

Brotherly Love
Faith of Our Fathers

Fear of the Lord
O Worship the King

Integrity
Living For Jesus

Joy
O, For a Thousand Tongues

Obedience - Trust and Obey

Responsibility
Give of Your Best

Virtue
Fairest Lord Jesus

Love - God's Grace
I Love to Tell the Story

Several books are available giving the background story of hymns. You may wish to use these to enrich your enjoyment. There are also many choruses (Sunday school-type songs) that are fun to sing and easy to learn. They can be found in many publications. We've listed some in the Resources Section.

Scripture for Memorization and Meditation

The life-changing study of God's Word begins with personal devotion to the Scripture: reading and listening, diligent memorization, and prayerful meditation. In most churches, homes, and schools, far too little attention has been given to the development of these disciplines in children's lives. Scripture meditation moves the child from passively listening to the telling of Bible stories, to the active role of thinking through the story and its application to his/her own life.

Portions to be memorized include:

- 1 Corinthians 13
- John 14:1-14
- Psalm 139
- Philippians 4:4-13
- Psalm 19
- Romans 12:3, 6-8
- Selected Proverbs
- Matthew 5:1-16
- Romans 8:28-39

Bible Facts

The Bible Facts are an attempt to summarize, in catechistic form, the Facts from important, larger sections of Scripture, or to collate important, related concepts from several different parts of Scripture. The implicit principles are more important than word-for-word Memorization (although the latter is encouraged). Older children should become familiar with the subject matter and be able to create new questions from the answers and meaningfully discuss the concepts involved.

The Bible Facts include:

- Matthew Eighteen Principle
- The Facts of Creation
- Books of the Bible
- The Beatitudes
- Great Christian Virtues
- The Ten Commandments
- Facts about Love
- Old Testament Prophecies of Christ
- Fruits and Gifts of God's Holy Spirit
- Facts about Salvation

Bible Passages for Study

Many Scripture Passages can be used for more than one Character Quality. We list several for each. You will, no doubt, be able to add to these

Projects and Activities

The Character Project is the heart of *Developing Godly Character in Children.* The purpose of each Project must always be to allow children to learn Biblical principles of Character growth in a practical, *hands-on* way. A successful Project is one in which a child is presented with an opportunity to choose God's way where previously he has been unaware of the choice, or where, indeed, he knowingly has chosen the world's way.

In other words, Character Projects are efforts to lift Bible study from a mere intellectual or emotional activity to a volitional one!

Developing Ideas for Character Projects:

They are birthed in the parent's own creativity as the parent keeps fresh in the Scripture and as he prayerfully seeks to discover the right Project for his children's present needs.

They are inspired by sharing with others informally, one-on-one, or in brainstorming sessions. One parent's casual suggestion may become another's high inspiration.

They grow out of any aspect of the *Developing Godly Character in Children* outline. In devising individual or group Projects, the parent will want to consider not only his child's needs, but also the various parts of the *Developing Godly Character in Children* outline. The project may stem from principles taught within the Key Verse or Working Definition, the Scripture Memorization, or the Bible Facts.

Projects can be integrated with almost any part of the academic curriculum:

HISTORY - the study of that Quality in lives of men and women of a certain period
LITERATURE – the value or non-value of great works and stories
LANGUAGE – sentence structure and diagramming, penmanship, vocabulary, spelling, creative writing projects related to the Quality
SCIENCE – study of collections of specimen; studying great men and women of science; creation science - all illustrating a certain aspect of God's character
THE ARTS - painting a Biblical or contemporary mural, dramatizing Scriptural passages, or composing character choruses, creative movement, making comic books, story boards, collages, drawings, paintings, and sculptures, using famous works of art, to spawn imaginative activities.

We reluctantly share specific examples for fear of stifling creativity through the inference that there is a limited number of "correct types" of Projects. In fact, the possibilities are a multiple of life experiences and subject areas taught; the several perspectives from which the curriculum outline views each Quality, and the extent of each parent's willingness to let his natural creativity arise. The project suggestions are shared, not as models to be copied, but rather as examples to spur parents to brain-storm for themselves and to discover from the depths of their own creativity, projects that will enable their children to be confronted with life-changing choices.

Projects and Activities best suited for groups larger than a typical family are designated by an asterisk (*).

Although the Projects and Activities are listed according to Character Qualities within the Units, ideas may be gained from listings other than the Character Quality currently being studied.

General Projects and Activities that may be used with most of the Unit Studies are listed on Page 125.

Resources

Each family needs to be very discerning when developing its collection of books, toys, videos, DVDs, CDs, and video games. Even computer links and favorites or bookmarks on one's computer should be guarded. Remember, what goes into a brain is filed there – graphically.

You will want to find books, videos, CDs, games, coloring books and other types of products to reinforce these lessons. Some good sources for materials are:

- Your Personal Library
- Bookstores: Christian and Secular
- Libraries: Church, Public, and Private
- Curriculum Suppliers: Home-School and Secular
- The Internet

If you have not already begun, we suggest you go through your collections, evaluate them and only keep those which are praiseworthy, and imaginative toward developing wisdom and creativity. This could be an on-going project.

We also recommend that you read or listen to each product before investing in it, and/or presenting it to your children. Just because you found material in a Christian bookstore, or on a website that seems to be Christian-based, does not mean the material will meet your standards.

Add to your collections great works of literature and culture, based upon how they will enrich your family – not just what entertains. Many great stories were penned by godly people, whether they became books or movies.

Buy and keep toys that foster thinking, creativity, imagination, not those that are based on movies, television programs, or today's wrong priorities and attitudes.

Indexing Resources

Here are some tips for organizing your Resource materials:

- Many family devotional books are set up with 1 or 2 page stories or scenarios with discussion following.
- Magazines targeted to parents/children/teachers often have valuable material applying to a number of the Character Qualities.
- Color code with high-lighters the Table of Contents of family devotional books, literature, reading books, and magazines targeted toward parents/children/teachers indicating which Character Quality a story or article deals with (e.g., light blue for Loyalty, pink for Love, etc.)
- If you are enterprising and organized you might want to set up a computer file with a section for each Quality and Resource, listing title of publication, title of story or article, page number, Character Qualities, etc.

Setting Goals

Someone has said that those who have no goals simply go in circles. Sometimes as parents we feel that way. You may want to clarify your parenting goals before proceeding. The following goals were defined by a group of parents who were committed to Christ and to one another to work to achieve in their families the ultimate goal in every part of life: finding and fulfilling God's purposes - for His glory and the highest good of each individual.

Goals for the Christian Family

- To develop complete unity between husband and wife in thought, attitude, and purpose.
- To develop in the household an atmosphere of God's presence which will influence all who enter.
- To develop in the children a reverence for God, His Word, His church, and His service which will enable them to live for Him when independent of the home's direct influence.
- To develop relationships by which each member of the family can have all physical, emotional and mental needs met.
- To fully develop each family member's potential in life by mutually honoring and nurturing one another's unique role and ministry.
- To develop freedom from bondage of all temporal values, including *credit living*.

Setting Goals for an Individual Child

Before introducing a Unit of Study, you will want to evaluate which Character Quality your child or family needs at that time.

You may study the Qualities in the order listed here; however, we recommend you look through the following Character Qualities list in order to discern where the greater needs are and select a Major Quality accordingly.

For example, if your child has been *slothful* you can look down the alphabetical negative list to find that its opposite falls under the Character Quality of *Responsibility*. You might choose that as your first Unit Study.

Taking time to evaluate areas of need in each child's life is an important aspect of planning for *Developing Godly Character in Children.* The following chart may help you think through the process.

Goals

Goals for:____
child's name

Date:____

Our/my **long range goals** for this child's character can be summarized by the following list or paragraph:____________________________________

Our/my **immediate goals** for this child's character (which I/we hope can be substantially met this year), and some of the methods I/we will use to reinforce them are:

Goals Methods of Reinforcement

Character Qualities
Negative and Positive

In sets of five for easy reading

Negative	Positive Counterpart	Unit Study
Aloofness	Friendliness	Brotherly Love
Anger	Meekness	Obedience
"	Yielding of Rights	Fear of the Lord
Anxiety	Trust	Faith
"	Security	Faith
Arrogance	Humility	Fear of the Lord
Apathy	Enthusiasm	Responsibility
Bitterness	Forgiveness	Brotherly Love
Callousness	Sensitivity	Virtue
"	Compassion	Brotherly Love
Conceit	Humility	Fear of the Lord
"	Reverence	Fear of the Lord
Contempt	Love	Brotherly Love
Contentiousness	Persuasiveness	Integrity
Covetousness	Contentment	Joy
Cowardice	Boldness	Fear of the Lord
Deceptiveness	Truthfulness	Virtue
Demanding Rights	Yielding of Rights	Fear of the Lord
Despondency	Hopefulness	Faith
Dishonesty	Truthfulness	Virtue
Disobedience	Obedience	Obedience
Disorganization	Orderliness	Responsibility
Disrespect	Reverence	Fear of the Lord
Distrust	Trusting	Faith
Doublemindedness	Courage	Faith
"	Decisiveness	Responsibility
Extravagance	Thriftiness	Responsibility
Faintheartedness	Endurance	Integrity
"	Determination	Fear of the Lord
Fearfulness	Boldness	Fear of the Lord
Fear of Man	Fear of God	Fear of the Lord

12 – Developing Godly Character in Children

Negative	Positive Counterpart	Unit Study
Foolishness	Wisdom	Wisdom
"	Cautiousness	Responsibility
Giving Up	Endurance	Integrity
Greed	Generosity	Brotherly Love
Immaturity	Maturity	Virtue
Immorality	Gentleness	Brotherly Love
Impatience	Patience	Virtue
Impurity	Purity	Virtue
Inattentiveness	Attentiveness	Obedience
Incompleteness	Thoroughness	Responsibility
Inconsistency	Consistency	Integrity
Indecisiveness	Boldness	Fear of the Lord
Indifference	Commitment	Loyalty
"	Compassion	Brotherly Love
Indiscretion	Discretion	Brotherly Love
Inflexibility	Flexibility	Faith
Injustice	Justice	Wisdom
Intolerance	Tolerance	Brotherly Love
Irresponsibility	Responsibility	Responsibility
Irresoluteness	Purposefulness	Faith
Jealousy	Trust	Faith
Judgment	Discernment	Wisdom
Loneliness	Friendliness	Brotherly Love
"	Hospitality	Brotherly Love
Natural Inclination	Wisdom	Wisdom
Negativism	Optimism	Faith
Neglect	Attentiveness	Obedience
Partiality	Fairness	Loyalty
Permissiveness	Firmness	Fear of the Lord
Prejudice	Tolerance	Brotherly Love
Presumption	Faith	Faith
Pride	Humility	Fear of the Lord
Rashness	Cautiousness	Responsibility
"	Deliberation	Fear of the Lord

Negative	Positive Counterparts	Unit Study
Rebelliousness	Respect for Authority	Fear of the Lord
"	Submissiveness	Obedience
Rejection	Faith	Faith
"	Forgiveness	Brotherly Love
Resentment	Acceptance	Brotherly Love
Resistance	Submission	Obedience
"	Flexibility	Faith
Rudeness	Deference	Brotherly Love
Scorn	Affirming	Fear of the Lord
Self-Centeredness	Availability	Fear of the Lord
Selfishness	Generosity	Virtue
"	Love	Brotherly Love
Self-Indulgence	Moderation	Moderation
Self-Pity	Joy	Joy
"	Thankfulness	Virtue
Skepticism	Belief	Faith
Sensuality	Purity	Wisdom
Simplemindedness	Discretion	Wisdom
Slander	Acceptance of Others	Brotherly Love
Slothfulness	Diligence	Responsibility
Stinginess	Generosity	Virtue
Stubbornness	Flexibility	Faith
Tardiness	Punctuality	Responsibility
"	Consideration	Brotherly Love
Timidity	Boldness	Fear of the Lord
Treachery	Loyalty	Loyalty
Unawareness	Alertness	Integrity
Unbelief	Belief	Faith
"	Faith	Faith
Uncleanness	Purity	Virtue
Unconcern	Compassion	Brotherly Love
Under-Achievement	Creativity	Joy
Ungratefulness	Gratefulness	Fear of the Lord
Unreliability	Responsibility	Responsibility
Unresponsiveness	Initiative	Responsibility
Wastefulness	Resourcefulness	Responsibility

Preparing a Unit of Study

A reproducible Lesson Plan Form is just inside the back cover of this book, to make it easy to fit into a copy machine. If you're using *Developing Godly Character in Children* at home or in a classroom, you'll need one lesson plan for each week. If you're using it weekly in a church setting, you'll need about one Lesson Plan per month.

Determine which Major Character Quality you are going to study.

Familiarize yourself with the material related to that Character Quality.

There are several resources for this understanding:

- The Scripture Passages: Meditate on the applicable references, related terms, opposites and abuses.
- The Character Quality Definitions: memorize for yourself the Definition of the Major Quality.
- Your Life Experiences: recount in your spirit and record in a life notebook the lessons you've learned about the particular Character Quality.
- Others' Life Experiences: continually share and encourage others to share within your support group or Christian community.

Determine your general goal for the Unit based on:

- The long-term goals of the parents
- The needs of the particular child
- The parents' inner awareness of God's specific direction
- A sample goal might be: "To have the child grow in his understanding and application of the Biblical teaching on Obedience."
- Referring to the list of Negative Qualities and their Positive Counterparts can be helpful to parents, role models, and students for use in identifying and overcoming such characteristics.

16 – Developing Godly Character in Children

Determine your approach for this Unit:

This will be determined by two things: your General Goals and the materials available to you. Evaluate material to develop ideas for Bible lessons and character-building Projects and Activities. If possible, participate in a creative brain-storming session with other parents using the material. If you're working alone, don't be discouraged. God is with you and will give you ideas and His anointing.

Identify measurable behavioral objectives:

Your general goal should now be clarified in terms of Measurable Behavioral Objectives, so that after the Unit is completed, you can evaluate the success of your work and write down insights for future planning. The following is a sample of objectives for a Unit of Study Obedience given in measurable terms:

- The children will have learned the Bible Memory material with 80% accuracy.
- The children will illustrate an understanding of the principles of Obedience in Peter's life by scoring at least 80% on a test given at the end of the Unit.
- The children will evidence an understanding of Submission through actions and attitudes.
- The children will evidence growth in their general attitude toward authority as demonstrated by significant, positive behavioral changes in 3 of 10 areas inventoried on surveys given before and after the Unit of study.
- The following is a sample test for evaluating a child's progress. It could be given at the beginning of a Unit of Study and again at the end. It may be taken by the child himself if he's old enough, or scored by the parent for a younger child.

I am more successful obeying my parents.
I receive B's or above on all work.
I do my chores without being asked.
I receive correction with a positive attitude.
I complete my schoolwork.
I keep my room clean.
I am more alert during class.
I seek forgiveness when I have offended others.
I share my feelings and experiences with my family.
I participate in discussions.
I have my "chores chart" signed.
I respond without anger when I am unjustly accused.
The incentive has influenced my behavior.
My goals have influenced my behavior.
I have gained other rewards from the goals.

Design a Project or Projects:

Based on the specific Behavioral Objectives you have for your children, plan a Project to reinforce the teaching. These Projects may grow out of the Memorization/Meditation, the Bible Facts, the Character Quality, or from the ideas listed in the Projects section. The objective is to find Projects which give practical definition and application to the child's needs. Some Projects may last only one day or one week; others may take the entire Unit Study period to complete.

Suggestions

- Based on the approach and objectives, select material from Scriptures and other resources to illustrate the principles of the Character Quality being studied.

- Pray for divine inspiration as you write lesson plans for the Unit.

- Each family will need to evaluate its own schedule and needs. We recommend a daily time with children to instruct, discuss, drill, and review material. If children are attending a classroom school, this could be during or after a meal, at the beginning of the day as a part of family devotions; as soon as the children return from school; or a time set aside before bedtime. Keeping the atmosphere light and upbeat will help children look forward to these times together.

- Choose a Scripture Passage to illustrate the Character Quality or Sub-Qualities. The selection will depend on the ages and interests of the children.

- Select a Project such as dramatic stories, puppetry, drama, discussion, art or craft. See Project Suggestions for idea starters.

Reminder: For your convenience, the Lesson Plan Form is located inside the back cover.

Discipline with Confidence

"Train up a child in the way he should go and when he is old he will not depart from it." Proverbs 22:6.

Discipline is not an option, nor is it punishment. It is an integral part of parenting. The Bible, especially the book of Proverbs has many references to the role parents play in the training of children. Following is a collection of thoughts concerning this broad subject.

Let's examine the way God dealt with the Children of Israel as an example of a Parent training His children. When Israel was a young nation He gave them the Law, with rules and consequences for breaking them. Understanding didn't come until much later. He knew that first, they had to learn His authority and justice. Yet all the while, it was with a Father's protective love and provision. When our children are small, we must give them rules and consequences as well, always with love.

When Israel reached the Promised Land, they were given responsibilities, along with the Law and consequences. This is how we should treat our children who are old enough to reason and handle responsibilities of maturity – about 6 – 18 years old.

It wasn't until Jesus came that the Law was fulfilled and internalized. Through Jesus' teachings on love, and the coming of the Holy Spirit, the church (Israel grown up) learned that she was to prepare herself as a grown-up bride. Freedom comes with grown-up understanding.

For Israel (the O.T. Church), Obedience is now to come from hearts of love and devotion rather than merely because of God's authority and Law. This is what we hope to ultimately accomplish in our own children, as they become more responsible to God and need us less.

Discipline Words to Know

Affection is warmth and kindness, in word and deed, which provides the atmosphere in which a child best responds to correction. Through affection, the child learns that he's lovable and has worth.

Appreciation communicates to the child that he has value. He sees his significance through the expressions of *affirmation* he receives, primarily from his parents, but from others as well.

Availability provides the child with a sense of importance. To a child, love equals time – time spent with the parent, doing things together, sharing the small and large parts of life.

20 – Developing Godly Character in Children

Structure may be provided so the child has the security of knowing in every activity

- Who is in authority
- Just what is expected of him
- What will happen in the event of either obedience or disobedience

Thus, a loving, caring parent or authority places a strong emphasis on the respect of rules. Rules, however, should only supplement the appreciation shown by the parent. The more affirmation the child receives when he does things right, the less correction he will need for doing wrong.

Reinforcement may be both positive (affirmation) and negative (punishment). Reward and punishment are used to reinforce proper behavior.

Positive reinforcement:

☺ ***Praise*** when effort is significant for the particular student.
☺ ***Acknowledgment*** before a peer group or respected elders when action is worthy of emulation.
☺ Added ***privilege*** and ***responsibility*** when the student shows himself responsible in smaller assignments.
☺ Material ***reward*** when previously announced as the reward for a longer-range project involving commitment and significant effort.
☺ A ***special time and activity*** with parent when the student has consistently responded to authority and love.

Negative Reinforcement:

☹ ***Verbal correction*** (eye to eye, soft-spoken, appealing to the child's sense of right and wrong), as often as needed and as often as possible!
☹ ***Withdrawal of privilege and responsibility*** when abused.
☹ ***Work assignment*** when the child's disobedience creates an added burden for others and the task can help him visualize this.
☹ ***Isolation*** when the child needs to cool down; when his repeated disruption makes meaningful group activity impossible.

Means of Reinforcement Never to Use

✂ Favoritism
✂ Unfulfilled promises (to reward or punish)
✂ Humiliation (serious punishment in front of peers, belittling language, etc.)
✂ Argumentation with child (Once you argue, you have moved below the child's peer level and you have lost ground.)
✂ Use of hands to punish: grabbing, poking, pushing, hitting (Hands are meant for loving.)
✂ Punishing in anger
✂ Punishing without adequate explanation
✂ Assigning homework as punishment

Use of Commendations

One of the best ways to instill Godly Character Qualities is to give positive reinforcement when a person displays them. The family setting is ideal for sharing the growth and progress of character development. The extended family and church community provide additional settings for Commendations.

It may seem awkward at first to speak with your children at length about actions and attitudes. Don't let the awkwardness prevent this worthy method of reinforcement. Adults and children will soon move beyond the awkwardness and look forward to such times of sharing.

If you are part of a church or home school support group, you may want to incorporate Commendation giving into your park-days, end-of-the-year program, or other gatherings. A church may incorporate such a time into informal potluck dinners, house fellowships, etc. You might include a time to present Certificates of Commendation at end-of-the-year programs, such as graduation or awards nights.

Two forms of positive reinforcement are verbal praise and written commendations. Either form should express praise or gratitude for specific action(s), or for reflecting consistency or growth in a given Character Quality.

Verbal commendations should . . .

be addressed in the first and second person ("I" and "you")
be eye-to-eye with the person commended.
use the child's name when you say . . . "**Congratulations!**"

Sample Verbal Commendation Reflecting Growth: "I want to commend you, Johnny, for consistency in the Character Quality of Obedience. Last week I watched you respond quickly to the request of the Sunday school teacher to help clean up the classroom. This response blessed both me and the teacher. It has been a joy for me to watch you, Johnny, consistently display an obedient spirit toward all in authority, both at home and church."

Sample Spoken Commendation Reflecting Growth: "I want to commend you, Sarah, for growth in the Character Quality of Generosity. In the past your sense of personal rights has sometimes caused you to overlook the needs of others, which you might have met through your many capabilities. So it was a happy moment this week when I spotted you giving up your favorite book when your friend, Kate, was visiting. Sarah, you not only shared your book, you also took the time to ask her how she enjoyed it when she had finished reading."

Written Commendations

- May be a hand-written note expressing thoughts similar to those above;
- May be written on a specially prepared form similar to a Certificate of Merit which would have blanks to be completed by parents;
- They could take the form of a poster or art work displayed on the family bulletin board.

Sample Written Commendations

Informal Note (on pillow, in lunch bag with sandwich, posted on refrigerator, stuck on a mirror, etc.)

Johnny,

Mom and I have been pleased to see the growth you've shown in the area of keeping your room tidy. The consistency and cheerfulness you've displayed has demonstrated your desire to accept responsibility. Keep up the good work.

Dad

Official-Looking Certificate (These can be made with a computer word processing program.) Sample wording:

Certificate

This is to Certify that

____

Child's Name

Has Demonstrated the Character Quality of

____

During the Month of

____

______________ ______________

Father *Mother*

Ten Steps of Correction

Remember that the first step in training young lives is to **decide** what behavior you want, then to **communicate** and **instruct** the child toward that behavior. **Correction** is to follow the breaking or violation of previously established **rules** or **guidelines** with the view toward forming appropriate behavior. Parents who are new to this way of consistent discipline have found that the children usually "test" the parent for at least three days to discover whether the parent will follow through. With love and patience, after the initial few days, life calms down and there's less often a test of wills. This can be an exhausting time for the parent, but if he /she is consistent, the child will soon learn resistance isn't worth the effort.

If you're new to this, you might want to introduce your motivation and new methods through a discussion of point five, before the first infraction of the rules.

1. Avoid embarrassment and outside interference. Get alone. Only with a very young child - who can't remember long enough to link the discipline to the offense - should discipline be dealt with publicly.

2. Establish responsibility for the disobedience. Ask, "What did you do that was wrong?" (Not *why?* But *what?*). Thc goal is to have the child mentally and verbally acknowledge hls responsibility.

3. Communicate grief over the offense. Your facial expression and words should convey your sorrow over the offense.

4. Associate love with correction. God's love *and* your own should be evident.

5. Establish God as the final authority. The parent is God's delegated authority over the child. However, make it your goal to instill in the child a desire to please God. Don't portray God as waiting to pounce on the offender.

6. Use a neutral object - not the hand. "Foolishness is bound in the heart of a child, but the rod of correction shall drive it far from him," (Proverbs 22:15).

7. With children old enough to reason: Discipline until godly sorrow is manifested. In children under age 4 or 5, discipline once, remove the child from temptation in order to change the child's train of thought. This teaches the child to turn from the temptation and change his behavior. Keep in mind that we all learn best when pain is associated with a wrong – whether the pain is physical or emotional.

8. Comfort the child after correction. A hug and kind words will communicate acceptance and unconditional love to the child.

9. Discuss any appropriate restitution. Establish the child's responsibility in the restitution. It may include scrubbing the crayon marks off the walls or working off the cost of a broken window.

10. Evaluate your correction and your child's response to it. Reflection will help prepare you for future disciplinary needs.

Parenting Types

Passive Parents have no rules. Anything the child wants to do is okay. There is very little - or perhaps, no - discipline. The Passive Parent's style is usually based on a lack of self-confidence as a parent. He feels threatened by the child's natural spontaneity, impulsiveness, and low tolerance for frustration. In order to avoid conflict with the child he appeases, indulges, and generally tries to maintain a state of bliss. The parent mistakenly thinks that conflict with the child means he will lose the child's love. The parent thinks he's allowing the child to grow on his own. However, the child thinks the parent is indifferent. The child doesn't get training in social skills, so becomes either shy, obnoxious, or self-centered. A child raised by Passive Parents generally lacks security, skills, and self-confidence.

Similar to the Passive Parent, the **Permissive Parent** is afraid of losing the child's love. While showering affection on the child, he fails to provide guidelines and limitations. In this home, the child makes most decisions because he quickly learns he can. The child raised by Permissive Parents will perhaps, know he is loved, yet lack skills and self-confidence.

Like the Passive or Permissive Parent, the **Authoritarian Parent** fears conflict with the child. He establishes a highly-structured, rule-governed life. The child learns to obey, not because he's learning how to conduct himself, but rather, to avoid the pain of punishment. Many such children discover that in the absence of an authority figure, they can get away with breaking rules. They don't develop self-discipline. Also, the child develops the concept that the parent's love is conditional upon the child keeping the rules. The child raised by Authoritarian Parents may learn social skills but often feels inadequate, unsure of whether he's living up to others' expectations, especially in situations where there are no specific rules. The child will have certain skills, yet lack security and self-confidence.

The **Affectionate-Mentoring Parent** communicates unconditional love and affection for the child. His love also includes guidelines (rules) and instructions in behavior (principles based on reasons). Such parents are self-confident, relaxed and firm in their management. The parent gradually gives the child increasingly more responsibility to make decisions based on the foundational information the parent has been providing. The child learns how to apply general principles to various situations. Such children learn to discipline themselves and to evaluate new situations where no guidelines are apparent. The child raised by Affectionate-Mentoring Parents develops security, skills and self-confidence.

Other Uses for this Material

Although the supportive material in this handbook is addressed to parents, the curriculum itself is well suited for use by both adults and young people. Other uses for this material include:

Group Studies

Sunday school classes, youth groups, even home Bible study and support groups, find the curriculum a resource for developing Godly Character in their lives. Several like-minded families can join together and share the Unit Studies.

With prayer, a little imagination, and adaptation, group leaders will find members enjoy the study of Character Qualities. Projects can be created to involve the entire group, such as repairing and painting the homes of senior citizens, gathering relief supplies for disaster victims, delivering food to the needy, etc.

Individual Study

A highly motivated individual will find this material valuable for personal study. New converts have used it as a guide to topical Bible study and application.

Resource Material for Sermons and Bible Lessons

Pastors and other speakers find the categorical listings valuable in preparing messages and lessons.

Children's Church and Classroom Schools

Although parents carry the primary responsibility of training their children, most families will at some time look to the church and/or school for assistance with this training. Keeping in mind that God has given parents the responsibility of training children, school and church workers will view themselves as extensions of the parental influence.

As such, the Christian church and/or school exists as an extension of, and a ministry to, the Christian home, assisting parents to build character in young lives.

The local church and school should work together to provide motivation, methods and materials for Christian parents to fulfill their responsibility.

Objectives for Classroom Teachers

This material was originally created for classroom use in Christian Schools. It can also be used in the Children's Church and Sunday School setting. When an entire Sunday school or student body studies the same Character Quality simultaneously, the benefits multiply. The following guidelines should be helpful:

Each Trimester - If three Character Qualities are studied each school year, the time period for a Unit would be called a trimester.

Study the learning material related to the Character Quality: Definitions, Key Verse, Memorization, Bible Facts.

Participate creatively in faculty brainstorming sessions to develop ideas for Bible lessons, class Meditation/Memorization activities, and character building Projects (each trimester or as assigned by the administrator).

Design a class Project. These Projects may grow out of the Scriptures for Memorization or Meditation, the Bible Facts, or the Character Quality in any sense which its "practical definition" applies to student needs, although the administrator may require one, two, or three Projects per year. It need not be considered crucial that a Project accompany each trimester's study.

Weekly - Keep personally current in your own mind and spirit by memorizing and meditating on the assigned verses and by learning the Bible Facts material.

Meet with a faculty prayer partner to agree concerning your needs, those of your classes, and of individual students.

Design lesson plans of class activities for the Meditation and the Project.

Daily - Pray for God's guidance in imparting principles from His Word to the students and pray for God's Spirit to rule in the class and in specific students' lives.

Occasionally as Assigned - Prepare all parts of chapel services (songs, recitations, testimonies, Bible lessons, etc.) around the Character theme.

Wisdom

These principles are so essential to creating happy, efficient homes and classrooms, we recommend this unit be taught during the **first** week of each school year.

Key Verses

WISDOM – For the Lord gives wisdom, and from his mouth come knowledge and understanding. Proverbs 2:6

DISCERNMENT - For God sees not as man sees, for man looks at the outward appearance, but the Lord looks at the heart. I Samuel 16:7

DISCRETION - The prudent sees the evil and hides himself, but the naive go on and are punished for it. Proverbs 22:3

JUSTICE - Administer true justice; show mercy and compassion to one another. Zechariah 7:9

Definitions

WISDOM is looking at life's situations from God's point of view.

DISCERNMENT is seeing through surface problems to root causes. *Power or faculty of the mind which distinguishes one thing from another, as truth from falsehood; virtue from vice; power of perceiving differences or ideas, and their relations and tendencies*

DISCRETION is thinking before I speak, remembering that my words can injure me or others. *That which enables a person to judge critically of what is correct and proper, united with caution; primarily concerned with one's own conduct (Webster quotes Proverbs 3:21).*

JUSTICE is demonstrating fairness to others even at my own expense. *Honest; conforming to the laws; True; founded in truth and fact; True to promises; Impartial; allowing what is due; giving fair representation of character, merit or demerit.*

Hymn

Just a Closer Walk with Thee

I am weak abut Thou art strong;
Jesus keep me from all wrong;
I'll be satisfied as long
As I walk, let me walk close to Thee.

Thru' this world of toil and snares,
If I falter, Lord, who cares?
Who with me my burden shares?
None but Thee, dear Lord, none but Thee.

When my feeble life is o'er,
Time for me will be no more;
Guide me gently, safely o'er
To Thy kingdom shore, to Thy shore.

Scripture for Memorization and Meditation

Selected Verses

Proverbs 1:9 – Listen my son, to your father's instruction and do not forsake your mother's teaching. They will be a garland to grace your head and a chain to adorn your neck.

Proverbs 3:13-18, 21 – Blessed is the man who finds wisdom, the man who gains understanding, for she is more profitable than silver and yields better returns than gold. She is more precious than rubies; nothing you desire can compare with her. Long life is in her right hand; in her left hand are riches and honor. Her ways are pleasant ways, and all her paths are peace. She is a tree of life to those who embrace her; those who lay hold of her will be blessed. My son, preserve sound judgment and discernment, do not let them out of your sight; they will be life for you, an ornament to grace your neck.

Proverbs 22:6 – Train a child in the way he should go, and when he is old he will not turn from it.

Bible Facts

1. **What is Wisdom not?** Wisdom is: not "being filled with knowledge."

2. **What is Wisdom?** Wisdom is looking at life's situation from God's point of view.

3. **How does Wisdom help me in my daily life?** When I learn God's unchangeable truths and life principles, and to know His character, I will be able to recognize falsehood or folly when it comes.

4. **Where does Wisdom come from?** Proverbs 2:6 says that, "The Lord gives wisdom, and from his mouth come knowledge and understanding."

5. **How is Wisdom worked out in one's life?** I do that by learning God's Word, the Bible, by learning to know His voice through prayer and meditation, and by studying knowledge under the guidance of godly people.

6. **What is man's wisdom?** Rather than wisdom, it is the gathering of philosophies, doctrines, and facts that are filtered and biased by the one teaching it.

7. **How does this difference affect my learning?** True sciences, whether the study of history, the environment, literature, philosophies, languages or culture, are based on God's unchangeable laws, and enables me to make wise decisions. Man's knowledge does not make one wise, only filled with facts and ideas.

Bible Passages for Study

Proverbs 3:13 - **Blessed is the man who finds wisdom**, the man who gains understanding,

Proverbs 9:12 - If you are wise, your **wisdom will reward you**; if you are a mocker, you alone will suffer."

Proverbs 13:10 - Pride only breeds quarrels, but **wisdom is found in those who take advice**.

Proverbs 15:33 - **The fear of the LORD teaches a man wisdom**, and humility comes before honor.

Proverbs 16:16 - How much **better to get wisdom than gold**, to choose understanding rather than silver!

Proverbs 19:8 - **He who gets wisdom loves his own soul**; he who cherishes understanding prospers.

Proverbs 19:11 - **A man's wisdom gives him patience**; it is to his glory to overlook an offense.

Proverbs 24:7 - **Wisdom is too high for a fool**; in the assembly at the gate he has nothing to say.

Proverbs 28:26 - He who trusts in himself is a fool, but he who walks in **wisdom** is kept safe.

Proverbs 29:15 - **The rod of correction imparts wisdom**, but a child left to himself disgraces his mother.

Ecclesiastes 9:18 - **Wisdom is better than weapons of war**, but one sinner destroys much good.

Luke 2:52 - And **Jesus grew in wisdom** and stature, and in favor with God and men.

Psalm 119:125 - I am your servant; **give me discernment** that I may understand your statutes.

Proverbs 17:10 - A rebuke impresses a man of **discernment** more than a hundred lashes a fool.

Job 34:4 - **Let us discern for ourselves what is right**; let us learn together what is good.

Philippians 1:10 - So that you may be **able to discern** what is best and may be pure and blameless until the day of Christ,

1 Chronicles 22:12 - **May the LORD give you discretion** and understanding when he puts you in command over Israel, so that you may keep the law of the LORD your God.

Proverbs 2:11 - **Discretion will protect you**, and understanding will guard you.

Proverbs 29:4 - **By justice a king gives a country stability**, but one who is greedy for bribes tears it down.

Proverbs 29:26 - Many seek an audience with a ruler, but **it is from the LORD that man gets justice**.

Proverbs 13:14, 20 – The teaching of the **wise** is a fountain of life, turning a man from the snares of death. He who walks with the **wise** grows wise, but a companion of fools suffers harm.

Projects and Activities

1. ✝ Begin a study of the book of Proverbs and categorize them. One chapter can be studied each day for a calendar month. On the first and last day, have each person write a description of a wise person and his traits. Afterwards compare the two descriptions.

2. ✝ The Mini-Unit of Wisdom might well be introduced by the parent sharing a significant part of his or her own life message with the children. A testimony that reveals important times of suffering or unpleasantness in his life introduces children to the fundamental principle of Wisdom ("God looks at my life as a unique expression of Christ's character").

3. *Wisdom* - Have guests in for dinner or an evening, who have a true-life story to share with the family showing the need to learn God's Wisdom in situations and that gaining such Wisdom can be fun. Keep the whole thing low-key and non-preachy.

4. *Wisdom* - Discuss the difference between man's knowledge and God's Wisdom.

5. *Wisdom* - Have the children develop a list for a *Wisest Person Award*. Ask Sunday school teachers, adult friends, and relatives, "Who is the wisest person you know?" "Why is he/she the wisest?"

6. *Discernment* - Use the Character Qualities - Negative and Positive list to create activities to
   - show how people have a tendency to see and expect the worst in others, whereas God sees our potential and our ultimate development of Character Qualities.
   - study synonyms and antonyms and the root words of the Character Qualities.
   - explore through various forms of art the emotions, body language, sign language, color and musical flavors of the Character Qualities.
   - explore the fact that these "heart words" are full of feelings but hard to describe. Realize that God searches our heart and knows our feelings.

7. *Discernment* - While studying art use word pictures. Have the child use a picture of himself and the name of an action and Character Quality into the picture or collage. This helps the child to identify his own Character Qualities.

8. *Wisdom* - Do an introductory study on the foundations and beginnings of modern sciences. Most fields were first studied by Renaissance Christians, Industrial Age or Modern Christians. As the Fathers of Science they desired to understand more of God's ordered creation.

9. *Wisdom* - Begin a personal collection of wise sayings in a special notebook.

10. *Wisdom* - Begin the habit of taking sermon notes. A bound “diary-type” of book serves this purpose nicely.

11. *Wisdom* - Do a study on the word “meditation” as described in the Bible.

12. *Discernment* - This is a good time to begin memory books or albums on each member of the family. Collect important achievements, events, things learned, steps of maturity noticed, milestones, proud moments, life lessons, anecdotes, cute observations. Have each member of the family assist the others in adding to their own collection.

A Parent's Prayer – A Paraphrase

We always thank God for you, our children, mentioning you in our prayers. We continually remember before God our Father how your faith is working, your love is growing, and your hope is enduring in your Lord Jesus Christ.

We know that you have been chosen by GOD, because our gospel comes to you not simply with words, but also with power, with the Holy Spirit, and with deep conviction. You know how we live with you day and night, choosing to train you at home for your sake. You are becoming imitators of us and the Holy Spirit. And so you become models to all onlookers in the community. Your faith in God has become known everywhere. Friends, relatives, and neighbors report of your service to God.

You know our decision to train you at home was not a mistake. With the help of God we dare to tell you His message despite many hardships. We are not trying to do things man's way, but we are confident our ways are approved by God who tests our hearts. We love you so much that we are delighted to share our lives with you, teaching you His ways, being gentle with you and caring for you because you are so dear to us.

We work hard at being good examples to you, while encouraging and comforting you, urging you to live lives worthy of God, who calls you into His kingdom and glory. We thank God continually, because you receive the message of God and He is working in you now. For what is our hope, our joy, or the crown of exultation in which we will glory in the presence of our Lord Jesus when He comes? Is it not you? Indeed, you are our glory and joy!

Now may the Lord make your love increase and overflow for each other and for everyone else, just as ours does for you. May He strengthen your hearts so that you will be faultless in purity in the presence of our God and Father. We instruct you, our children, how to live in order to please God, as in fact you are living; we urge you to do so more and more. You should be holy, and learn to control your desires in a way that is pure and honorable, not as the ungodly do. No one should wrong his brother or take advantage of him. Make it your ambition to lead a quiet life, to mind your own business, and to work with your hands at becoming self-sufficient, so that your daily life may win the respect of others and so that you will not depend on anybody.

Encourage each other about the Good News of Christ and the life we will live with Him. And live in such a way so that you will not be surprised at His coming. Respect those who work hard among you in the different ministries, and also those who are over you in the Lord, who admonish you. Hold them in the highest regard in love because of their work. Live at peace with each other, warn those who are idle, encourage the timid, help the weak, be patient with everyone.

Make sure that nobody pays back wrong for wrong, but always try to be kind to each other. Be joyful always; pray continually; give thanks in all circumstances, for this is God's will for you in Christ Jesus. Do not put out the Spirit's fire in your hearts or in another's. Hold on to the good around you and avoid every kind of evil.

May God Himself - the God of peace - clean you through and through. May your whole spirit, soul, and body be kept blameless at the coming of our Lord Jesus. The One who called you is faithful and He will do it.

Adapted by Debbie Peterson from St. Paul's letter to the church at Thessalonica, ©1996

Loyalty

These principles are so essential to creating happy homes and classrooms, we recommend this unit be taught during the **second** week of each school year – **after** a week on Wisdom.

Key Verses

LOYALTY - Do not judge lest you be judged yourselves. Matthew 7:1

COMMITMENT - But just as He who called you is holy, so be holy in all you do; for it is written; "Be holy, because I am holy." I Peter 1:15, 16

FAIRNESS - And just as you want men to treat you, treat them in the same way. Luke 6:31

FAITHFULNESS - Whoever can be trusted with very little can also be trusted with much, and whoever is dishonest with very little will also be dishonest with much. Luke 16:10

Definitions

LOYALTY is telling others only good about my friends and leaders, especially when I have been upset with them.

COMMITMENT is saying "yes" to God's goals for me, especially each time I realize how much they will cost me. *Pledging or engaging*

FAIRNESS is thinking carefully about everybody's needs before I make a decision; not choosing a certain way because I like or dislike someone.

FAITHFULNESS is seeing with my heart what God's goals are and working for them, even though I can't see them with my eyes. *Constant in the performance of duties or service.*

Hymn

Blest Be the Tie that Binds

Blest be the tie that binds
Our hearts in Christian love!
The fellowship of kindred minds
Is like to that above.

We share our mutual woes,
Our mutual burdens bear;
And often for each other flows
The sympathetic tear.

When we asunder part
It gives us inward pain;
But we shall still be joined in heart,
And hope to meet again.

Scripture for Memorization and Meditation

Psalm 139

1-3 - O Lord, you have searched me and you know me. You know when I sit and when I rise; you perceive my thoughts from afar. You discern my going out and my lying down; you are familiar with all my ways.

4-6 - Before a word is on my tongue you know it completely, O Lord. You hem me in - behind and before; you have laid your hand upon me. Such knowledge is too wonderful for me, too lofty for me to attain.

7-10 - Where can I go from your Spirit? Where can I flee from your presence? If I go up to the heavens, you are there; if I make my bed in the depths, you are there. If I rise on the wings of the dawn, if I settle on the far side of the sea, even there your hand will guide me, your right hand will hold me fast.

11-12 - If I say, "Surely the darkness will hide me and the light become night around me," even the darkness will not be dark to you; the night will shine like the day, for darkness is as light to you.

13-14 - For you created my inmost being; you knit me together in my mother's womb. I praise you because I am fearfully and wonderfully made; your works are wonderful, I know that full well.

15-16 - My frame was not hidden from you when I was made in the secret place. When I was woven together in the depths of the earth, your eyes saw my unformed body. All the days ordained for me were written in your book before one of them came to be.

17-18 - How precious to me are your thoughts, O God! How vast is the sum of them! Were I to count them, they would out number the grains of sand. When I awake I am still with you.

23-24 – Search me, O God, and know my heart; test me and know my anxious thoughts. See if there is any offensive way in me, and lead me in the way everlasting.

Bible Facts

* See Note to Parents on following page.

1. **How does God see our family?** God sees our family as a community assisting one another to grow in the character of His Son. Philippians 2:1-4 *"If you have any encouragement from being united with Christ, if any comfort from his love, if any fellowship with the Spirit, if any tenderness and compassion, then make my joy complete by being like-minded, having the same love, being one in spirit and purpose. Do nothing out of selfish ambition or vain conceit, but in humility consider others better than yourselves. Each of you should look not only to your own interests, but also to the interests of others. Your attitude should be the same as that of Christ Jesus."*

2. **What is my part in this community?** Our family is a community - different from the civil community - with a special goal. All my words and deeds should assist others to grow in the character of Christ. Ephesians 4:2, 3, 15, 16 *"Be completely humble and gentle; be patient, bearing with one another in love. Make every effort to keep the unity of the Spirit through the bond of peace…instead, speaking the truth in love, we will in all things grow up into him who is the Head, that is, Christ. From him the whole body, joined and held together by every supporting ligament, grows and builds itself up in love, as each part does its work."*

3. **What should I do to assist another if I observe him doing wrong?** Matthew 18:15 says that I should go to him alone and point out his error in a spirit of meekness.

4. **What actions should I expect from the one doing wrong?**
   - If breaking a rule, he should acknowledge his wrong and stop.
   - If offending another, he should seek forgiveness.
   - If stealing or damaging property, he should report his misdeed to the one in authority and make restitution.

5. **What if he will not hear me and will not take the necessary steps of action?** Matthew 18:16 says that I should ask him to go with me to the responsible authority. If he will not, I should bring the responsible authority to him and repeat the matter in the presence of both.

6. **How can the way I speak of others especially assist their growth?** James 4:11 teaches me that I will assist others' growth as I purpose not to speak evil about anyone, unless: I am speaking to him alone; in a loving way; and with the purpose of assisting him to grow.

7. **What should I do if others begin to speak evil of someone else?** I should ask them, please, not to continue; and I should refuse to listen.

8. **What is the Golden Rule and where is it found?** The golden rule, found in Matthew 7:12, says that *"whatever you want others to do for you, do so for them, for this is the law and the prophets."*

Note to Parents

The concepts presented in this section may at first seem unlikely to succeed. However, we have seen them work within families, in the neighborhood context within church congregations, and on Christian school campuses. In the Bible Facts section, use the questions to trigger discussion and explore these concepts. The answers to the questions can be memorized as catechistic material, or used as a basis for study.

God gave us our family first in order to be a training ground to learn and practice His principles. We need to master relationships at home before we can become successful with others.

Let the children come up with their own ideas, then guide them to the idea of the family as a community. Discuss and research how a community works (a city or village) and how the different jobs and departments rely on one another.

The parent should not listen to *bad reports* (tattling) about those not in their presence, even their own children. The parent should not permit children to report out loud what others are doing wrong, nor to make any negative comments regarding assigned work (murmuring) - or Mom's cooking, or brother's artwork, etc. (a *bad report* on another person). The parent should softly, firmly cut such comments short and deal with the offender alone, at a later time.

The parent should ask the *bearer of information about another's misdeed* (tattler) if he went alone first, and if he did, should discern whether he went in a spirit of meekness. If not, this must also be dealt with.

The obvious exception to the above is when there is immediate physical danger to another. In this case the parent should first remove the danger, then deal with the individuals.

Since *name-calling* and *put-downs* are the most common form of *evil speaking* among children, the parent should find out what each child wishes to be called (given names or nick names); instruct children on the importance of one's name, and enforce the rule that each is to be called nothing else at any time. In many homes, affectionate nick names are common. Of course, if the child likes the nick names, they may be used as well.

The parent should take care to correctly model this behavior:

Do you criticize the pastor, or his sermon?
Do you gossip about another's misfortune?
Do you and your friends enjoy the teasing form of *put-downs* and *jabs*?
Do you talk about your spouse in a way that makes yours look bad?

Bible Passages for Study

1 Samuel 24:6-10 – David's Loyalty to Saul
2 Samuel 1:14 – David's Loyalty when Saul Died
2 Samuel 11:9 – Uriah's Loyalty
2 Samuel 15:21 – Attai's Loyalty
2 Samuel 17:15, 16 – Hushai's Loyalty
2 Samuel 18:12:, 13, 23 – Loyalty of David's Soldiers
2 Samuel 19:32 – Boaz's Loyalty
2 Samuel 19:32 - Barzillai's Loyalty
2 Kings 11:4-12 – Jehoiada's Loyalty
Esther 2:21-23 – Mordecai & Esther

1 Kings 12:20 - When all the Israelites heard that Jeroboam had returned, they sent and called him to the assembly and made him king over all Israel. **Only the tribe of Judah remained loyal to the house of David.**

Galatians 5:22 - But the fruit of the Spirit is love, joy, peace, patience, kindness, goodness, **faithfulness**

3 John 1:3 - It gave me great joy to have some brothers come and tell about your **faithfulness** to the truth and how you continue to walk in the truth.

Revelation 13:10 - If anyone is to go into captivity, into captivity he will go. If anyone is to be killed with the sword, with the sword he will be killed. This calls for patient endurance and **faithfulness** on the part of the saints.

Proverbs 20:6 - Many a man claims to have unfailing love, **but a faithful man who can find?**

Proverbs 28:20 - **A faithful man will be richly blessed**, but one eager to get rich will not go unpunished.

Matthew 24:45 - "Who then is the **faithful** and wise servant, whom the master has put in charge of the servants in his household to give them their food at the proper time?

Matthew 25:21 - "His master replied, 'Well done, good and **faithful** servant**! You have been faithful with a few things**; I will put you in charge of many things. Come and share your master's happiness!'

1 Corinthians 4:2 - Now it is required that those who have been given a trust must prove **faithful.**

Projects and Activities

1. *Loyalty* - Talk together about a recent situation the group experienced or witnessed where tattling was accepted as normal. Discuss how things would have turned out if Matthew 18:15-17 had been practiced.

2. *Loyalty* - Together, write a covenant in which each person commits to practice Loyalty in word and in action.

3. *Fairness* - Write a skit and present it to children's church or youth group demonstrating how to handle relationship problems

4. *Loyalty/Fairness* - Discuss how wars between nations or people groups are the result of failing to practice Biblical principles of Loyalty.

5. *Fairness* - Interview someone who is known for *keeping the peace* with others. Discover their methods.

6. The parent can wear a red construction paper heart – for a day or even a week. Each time a hurtful thing is spoken about someone, the parent tears off a portion of the heart, using an expression of sorrow. Explain that this is what happens emotionally to the one spoken about and to the heart of God.

7. Explain the importance of *a good name* or one's reputation. Cut out the shape of a body on blank white paper. Tape it to a wall. Each time a bad report is spoken, demonstrate that the reputation is tarnished by making a big dark spot on the body. Explain that those who heard the report will now always see in their minds that tarnished mark when they think of that person.

8. *Loyalty* - Recite: "Sticks and stones can break my bones, but words can never hurt me." Explain that the quote is false because words really can and do hurt the heart.

9. *Fairness* - Act out situations from this unit's Bible Facts. When the situation demonstrates a wrong done to someone, have the one who did the wrong put an erasable mark on the wronged person's body. Have them act out the proper responses for restoration. Discuss why the words, "Will you forgive me?" are needed by both the offender and the offended. Sometimes it's best not to detail the disloyalty. Words such as "I haven't love you as I should. Will you forgive me?" might be better.

11. *Commitment/Faithfulness* - Have the children think about those they need to ask forgiveness of. Then teach them how to do it. This helps clear up much tension within homes and classrooms. An adult will be modeling Christ's heart when he or she asks forgiveness for wrongly accusing a child. One teacher says his most common error is putting a child down in front of students. He points out that this requires an apology in front of the entire class.

12. *Commitment/Faithfulness* - Spend an English lesson writing letters asking for forgiveness: of one another, of parents, of siblings.

13. *Fairness* - Have the children act out real-to-life situations and assist them to verbalize proper responses in their vocabulary and sentence structure, unique to their age levels. E.g., "It hurt me when you said that about my drawing." "I'm sorry, will you forgive me?"

14. *Fairness* - Deal with the "I'm sorry" cop-out. We have found that "I'm sorry," is often lightly thrown out as a way of ending a disagreement. Have the child look the other one in the eye and ask forgiveness, "I'm sorry I... (naming the offense), will you forgive me?" Parental modeling of appropriate 'forgiveness asking' is the best way to teach this principle.

Brotherly Love

Key Verses

LOVE – By this all men will know that you are my disciples, if you love one another. John 13:35

ACCEPTANCE OF OTHERS - Accept one another, then, just as Christ accepted you, in order to bring praise to God. Romans 15:7

AFFECTION - Be devoted to one another in brotherly love. Romans 12:10

AFFIRMATION - Each of us should please his neighbor for his good, to build him up. Romans 15:2

COMPASSION - If anyone has material possessions and sees his brother in need but has no pity on him, how can the love of God be in him? 1 John 3:17

DEFERENCE - Honor one another above yourselves. Romans 12:10

Definitions

LOVE is always wanting the best to happen to others.

ACCEPTANCE OF OTHERS is overlooking the differences of appearance, performance or opinion of another for the sake of harmony.

AFFECTION is being able to have and express feelings of love and acceptance of another.

AFFIRMATION is expressing to another the value I place on him and why. *To declare the existence of something.*

COMPASSION is feeling others' hurts enough to do something for them which may not be convenient for me. *Suffering with another; experiencing a sensation of sorrow excited by the distress or misfortunes of another (Webster quotes Psalm 78:38).*

DEFERENCE is limiting my freedom in order not to offend the personal taste of those I'm serving. *A yielding of opinion; submission of judgment to the opinion or judgment of another; respect.*

ENCOURAGEMENT - Therefore, encourage one another and build each other up, just as in fact you are doing. 1 Thessalonians 5:11

ENCOURAGEMENT is being able to lift the spirits of one who is discouraged.

FORGIVENESS - Be kind and compassionate to one another, forgiving each other, just as in Christ God forgave you. Ephesians 4:32

FORGIVENESS is helping heal a person who has wronged me by treating and speaking of him the same way I would if he had done no wrong.

FRIENDLINESS - He who has friends must show himself friendly. Proverbs 18:24

FRIENDLINESS is pressing beyond my sense of awkwardness to make another feel comfortable.

GENTLENESS - But we were gentle among you, like a mother caring for her little children. 1 Thessalonians 2:7

GENTLENESS is expressing personal care appropriate to another's emotional need.

HOSPITALITY - Do not forget to entertain strangers, for by so doing some have entertained angels without knowing it. Hebrews 13:2

HOSPITALITY is cheerfully sharing food, shelter, and spiritual refreshment with those God brings into my life.

PATIENCE - And not only so, but we also rejoice in our sufferings; because we know that suffering produces perseverance; and perseverance, character; and character, hope. Romans 5:3,4

PATIENCE is accepting a difficult situation from God without giving Him a deadline to remove it. *A calm temper which bears evils without murmuring.*

TOLERANCE - Make my joy complete by being of the same mind, maintaining the same love, united in spirit intent on one purpose. Philippians 2:2

TOLERANCE is accepting others as the Lord accepts me, remembering that He is not finished perfecting them or me. *The power or capacity of enduring discomfort.*

Hymn

And Can It Be?

And can it be that I should gain
An interest in the Savior's blood?
Died He for me, who caused His pain,
For me, who Him to death pursued?

He left His Father's home above,
So free, so infinite His grace!
Emptied Himself of all but love,
And bled for Adam's helpless race!

'Tis mercy all, immense and free,
For, O my God, it found out me.
Amazing love, how can it be,
That Thou, my God, shouldst die for me!

~ Chorus ~

Amazing love! How can it be?
That Thou, my God, shouldst die for me?
Amazing love! How can it be?
That Thou, my God, shouldst die for me?

Scripture for Memorization and Meditation

I Corinthians 13

1 - If I speak in the tongues of men and angels, but have not love, I am only a resounding gong or a clanging cymbal.

2 - If I have the gift of prophecy and can fathom all mysteries and all knowledge, and if I have a faith that can remove mountains, but have not love, I am nothing.

3 - If I give all I possess to the poor and surrender my body to the flames, but have not love, I gain nothing.

4-5 - Love is patient, love is kind. It does not envy, it does not boast, it is not proud. It is not rude, it is not self-seeking, it is not easily angered, it keeps no record of wrongs.

6-7 - Love does not delight in evil, but rejoices with the truth. It always protects, always trusts, always hopes, always perseveres.

8 - Love never fails. But where there are prophecies, they will cease; where there are tongues, they will be stilled; where there is knowledge, it will pass away.

9-10 - For we know in part and we prophesy in part, but when perfection comes, the imperfect disappears.

11 - When I was a child, I talked like a child, I thought like a child, I reasoned like a child. When I became a man, I put childish ways behind me.

12-13 - Now we see but a poor reflection; then we shall see face to face. Now I know in part; then I shall know fully, even as I am fully known. And now these three remain: faith, hope and love. But the greatest of these is love.

Bible Facts

The Elements of Love

1. **What is love not?** Love is not appreciating the good in another; it is not seeking or gaining another's approval; and it is not dependent upon being loved in return.

2. **What is love?** Love is wanting the best for another without regard for my own.

3. **How will love for another affect my life?** Love has the commitment to do good to another to the extent that I am able: Galatians 6:10, *"As we have opportunity, let us do good to all people."*

4. **How will the other person's feelings or attitudes toward me affect my love for him?** Because love is impartial , I will continue to want the highest good for that person regardless of his attitude toward me. *"Love your enemies, do good to those who hate you,"* Luke 6:27.

5. **Can I love someone I don't know and have never met?** I can love every person because I can commit myself to each one's highest good if ever given the opportunity to meet it.

6. **Are my neighbor's well being and feelings more valuable than my own?** No, we are of equal value. Jesus said, *"Love the Lord your God with all your heart and with all your soul and with all your strength and with all your mind, and, love your neighbor as yourself," Luke 10:27.*

7. **How can I know that I am truly loving another person?** I can treat him in a way that if I traded places with him, I know I wouldn't feel cheated by him: Luke 6: 31, *"Do to others as you would have them do to you."*

Bible Passages for Study

Luke 10:25-37 - The Good Samaritan
Luke 15:11-32 - The Prodigal Son
Luke 7:11-16 - The Widow Whose Only Son Had Died
John 8:1-11 - The Adulterous Woman
Matthew 14, John 6 - The Boy Who Shared His Lunch
Matthew 19:16-30 - The Rich Young Ruler
Matthew 19:13-15 - The Children
Genesis 28 and 29 - Jacob and Rachel
Ruth 1-4 - Naomi and Ruth
I Samuel 18-20 - David and Jonathan
Psalm 139 - We're Each Wonderfully Made
Proverbs 17:17 - Lending to the Lord
Matthew 27:31-58; Mark 15:20-45; Luke 23:26-52;
John 19:16-38 - Jesus' Seven Words from the Cross
Acts 4:30-35 - All Things in Common
Acts 20:17-38 - Love Between Paul and the Ephesians
Philemon - The Apostle's Love for a Runaway Slave
I John 3 - A Plea for Love Among the Brethren

John 13:35 - By this all men will know that you are my disciples, if you **love one another.**

Romans 12:10 - **Be devoted to one another in brotherly love**. Honor one another above yourselves.

Gal 5:13 - You, my brothers, were called to be free. But do not use your freedom to indulge the sinful nature; rather, **serve one another in love**.

Ephesians 4:2 - Be completely humble and gentle; be patient, bearing with **one another in love.**

Hebrews 10:24 - And let us consider how we may **spur one another on toward love** and good deeds.

1 Peter 1:22 - Now that you have purified yourselves by obeying the truth so that you **have sincere love for your brothers, love one another deeply**, from the heart.

Philippians 2:1- If you have any encouragement from being united with Christ, if any comfort from his love, if any fellowship with the Spirit, if any tenderness and **compassion...**

Colossians 3:12 - Therefore, as God's chosen people, holy and dearly loved, clothe yourselves with **compassion**, kindness, humility, gentleness and patience.

2 Timothy 4:2 - Preach the Word; be prepared in season and out of season; correct, rebuke and encourage--with great **patience** and careful instruction.

Titus 2:6 Similarly, **encourage** the young men to be self-controlled.

Hebrews 10:25 - Let us not give up meeting together, as some are in the habit of doing, but let us **encourage one another**--and all the more as you see the Day approaching.

Matthew 6:12, 14-15 - **Forgive** us our debts, as we also have forgiven our debtors. For if you forgive men when they sin against you, your heavenly father will also forgive you. But if you do not forgive men their sins, your Father will not forgive your sins.

Matthew 18:21 - Then Peter came to Jesus and asked, "Lord, how many times shall I **forgive my brother** when he sins against me? Up to seven times?"

Matthew 18:35 - "This is how my heavenly Father will treat each of you unless you **forgive your brother from your heart**."

Proverbs 15:1 - **A gentle answer turns away wrath**, but a harsh word stirs up anger.

1 Timothy 3:3 - …not given to drunkenness, not violent but **gentle**, not quarrelsome, not a lover of money.

Titus 1:8 - Rather he must **be hospitable**, one who loves what is good, who is self-controlled, upright, holy and disciplined.

Proverbs 15:18 - A hot-tempered man stirs up dissension, **but a patient man calms a quarrel.**

Proverbs 16:32 - **Better a patient man** than a warrior, a man who controls his temper than one who takes a city.

1 Corinthians 13:4 - **Love is patient**, love is kind. It does not envy, it does not boast, it is not proud.

Ephesians 4:2 - Be completely humble and **gentle**; **be patient**, bearing with one another in love.

Projects and Activities

1. *Brotherly Love/Compassion* - 1 Corinthians 13 offers many opportunities to identify word pictures, such as "clanging cymbal," "moving mountains," etc. Personalize it by replacing the name of the child for the word "I". Find the negatives such as, "I have a problem with:... boldness, or, delighting in evil."

2. *Encouragement/Affirmation* - Have the children give each other commendations. Most children cherish something that displays his name and something positive about him.

3. *Affirming* - *If Valentines Day comes in this time period, have the children make a valentine naming a favorite Character Quality in each child. Write 25 or so of these on the board and have the children write on each other's large paper heart.

4. *Brotherly Love* - Study the various types of love: *agape*, *phileo*, and *eros*. (The Greek has four words, only these three occur in the New Testament.)

5. *Compassion/Gentleness* - *For small children, pin a large, red heart on each child. During the day, tear off a chunk with each hurt the child receives. At the end of the day children will be able to see that what they do affects each other.

6. *Compassion/Affirmation* - Do a study of how words can build up or tear down. A review of the activities of the Loyalty unit might be useful.

7. *Affirmation/Compassion* - Talk about the harm of belittling comments and forbid their use. When teachers and parents forbid it in the classroom and home, it flows over into the rest of life.

8. *Forgiveness/Compassion* - Use art and drama to demonstrate forgiveness.

9. *Brotherly Love/Compassion* - Study Compassion as part of Brotherly Love: then act out the Good Samaritan story.

10. *Friendliness/Hospitality/Affection* - Create personalized gift wrap paper showing love for others, using hearts, etc.

11. *Acceptance of Others/Compassion/Friendliness/Hospitality* - Adopt a lonely grandparent, perhaps from church. Offer transportation and invitations to your home for "tea." Ask him/her to teach the family a skill or hobby.

12. *Hospitality/Compassion/Friendliness* - Find a needy person (or family) in your church or neighborhood. Surprise him with a special expression of love such as taking him out for

fresh fruit pie or filling a basket with goodies and leaving it on his doorstep. Discuss with the children the importance of protecting another person's dignity and feelings.

13. *Encouragement* - Make a Valentine Box by decorating a shoebox and adding a slit in the lid. Encourage family members to write compliments to one another (and the parents). Prepare a special meal with appropriate table settings. After dessert, open the box and read the notes to one another.

14. *Encouragement/Friendliness/Hospitality/Compassion* - Make "personal coupon books." Use 3 x 5 cards or construction paper with each page good for redeeming a non-cash gift of love: hug, back rub, chore, read aloud story, etc. Each page is written and signed by the person offering the love gift.

15. ✝ *Acceptance of Others* -*After studying God's nature, a group created a multimedia presentation using three projectors. They learned the reason we care for one another, and respect one another, is that we have a common creator - God.

16. *Hospitality/Friendliness* - Ask your church leadership if your family can be the church greeters for one month. Look for ways to show hospitality, friendliness, and gentleness to visitors and regular attendees.

17. *Affirming/Affection* - Volunteer as a family at a rest home, convalescent home, or school for handicapped for one month. Ask God to show you how to show His love.

18. *Hospitality*/Compassion - Go through your family's church, school, or home directory. Ask God to show you someone who might benefit from being shown hospitality and compassion. Invite them to dinner.

19. Hospitality/Compassion/Friendliness - Using the preceding idea, pick a secret pal. Encourage and affirm that one through cards, gifts, and calls.

20. *Compassion* - Become a sponsor for a third world child. Pray for him, write to her, etc.

21. *Hospitality/Friendliness* - Develop a weekly "Hospitality Night." Have family members take turns being the host for the evening. Other roles: door greeter; phone greeter; meal preparer; table decorator/setter.

22. *Acceptance of Others/Affirming/Encouragement/Patience* - Study the "Five Love Languages" as taught by Gary Smally. Find out what each family member's love language is. Discuss your findings and how this can help you give and receive love better within your family. Discuss how you can learn to recognize other's love language and meet their needs as well.

Reminder: There are General Suggestions for Projects and Activities listed on Page 125 that may apply to this Unit Study.

Faith

Key Verses

FAITH - Without faith it is impossible to please God, because anyone who comes to Him must believe that He exists and that He rewards those who earnestly seek Him. Hebrews 11:6

ADAPTABILITY - I have learned to be content whatever the circumstances. Philippians 4:11

BELIEF – If you confess with your mouth, "Jesus is Lord," and believe in your heart that God raised him from the dead, you will be saved. For it is with your heart that you believe and are justified, and it is with your mouth that you confess and are saved. Romans 10:9,10

CONFIDENCE - For the Lord will be your confidence and will keep your foot from being snared. Proverbs 3:26

COURAGE - I eagerly expect and hope that I will in no way be ashamed, but will have sufficient courage so that now as always Christ will be exalted in my body, whether by life or by death. Philippians 1:20

FLEXIBILITY - Set your minds on things above, not on earthly things. Colossians 3:2

Definitions

FAITH is seeing with my heart what God's goals are, and working for them, even though I can't see them with my eyes.

ADAPTABILITY is changing my actions or attitudes to fit the need. *That which is suitable.*

BELIEF is accepting with my heart that which cannot be proven with the senses. *A persuasion of the truth, or an assent of mind to the truth of a declaration, proposition or alleged fact, on the ground of evidence, distinct from personal knowledge.*

CONFIDENCE is belief in the truth of a fact, or in the integrity of another. *An assurance of mind or firm belief in the integrity or stability of another, or in the truth and reality of a fact.*

COURAGE is doing what I know is right when I think my friends will disagree or make fun of me or in an emergency I know my help is needed. *That quality of mind which enables men to encounter danger and difficulties with firmness.*

FLEXIBILITY is not setting my affections on plans which may be changed by others.

HOPEFULNESS - We continually remember before our God and Father your work produced by faith, your labor prompted by love, and your endurance inspired by hope in our Lord Jesus Christ. 1 Thessalonians 1:3

HOPEFULNESS is looking forward to something with peaceful anticipation. *Having a desire of some good, accompanied with at least a slight expectation of obtaining it, or a belief that it is obtainable; Confidence of a future event.*

OPTIMISM - Finally, brothers, whatever is true, whatever is noble, whatever is right, whatever is pure, whatever is lovely, whatever is admirable - if anything is excellent, or praise-worthy - think about such things. For as a man thinks within himself, so he is. Philippians 4:8,

OPTIMISM is choosing to believe that everything that affects me is ordered for God's glory and my ultimate good. *The opinion or doctrine that everything in nature is ordered for the best; the order of things in the universe that is adapted to produce the most good.*

PERSEVERANCE - Therefore, my dear brothers, stand firm. Let nothing move you. Always give yourselves fully to the work of the Lord, because you know that your labor in the Lord is not in vain. 1 Corinthians 15:58

PERSEVERANCE is sticking with a project or friend even when circumstances make it difficult. *Persistence in anything undertaken.*

PURPOSEFULNESS - Never be lacking in zeal, but keep your spiritual fervor, serving the Lord. Romans 12:11

PURPOSEFULNESS is avoiding activities that will distract me, and keeping to the goals the Lord and my leaders have given me. *Having intent and resolution.*

SECURITY - Do not work for food that spoils, but for food that endures to eternal life; which the Son of Man will give you. On Him God the Father has placed His seal of approval. John 6:27.

SECURITY is building my life around what is eternal and cannot be destroyed or taken away. *Freedom from fear or apprehension; confidence of safety.*

SELF-CONFIDENCE - I can do everything through Him Who gives me strength. Philippians 4:13

SELF-CONFIDENCE is recognizing that God made me at 100% of my potential, full of abilities, strengths and talents.

TRUSTING - Trust in the Lord with all your heart and lean not on your own understanding. Proverbs 3:5

TRUSTING is believing in the integrity of another. *Confiding in; giving credit; relying on.*

Hymn

Faith of Our Fathers

Faith of our fathers living still
In spite of dungeon, fire and sword;
O how our hearts beat high with joy
Whene'er we hear that glorious Word:

Our fathers chained in prisons dark
Were still in heart and conscience free;
How blest would be their children's fate
If they, like them, could die for Thee.

Faith of our fathers! We will love
Both friend and foe in all our strife;
And preach thee, too, as love knows how,
By kindly words and virtuous life.

~ Chorus ~

Faith of our fathers, holy faith;
We will be true to Thee till death.

Scripture for Memorization and Meditation

John 14:1-14

1-2 - "Do not let your hearts be troubled. Trust in God; trust also in me. In my Father's house are many rooms; if it were not so, I would have told you. I am going there to prepare a place for you."

3-4 - "And if I go and prepare a place for you, I will come back and take you to be with me that you also may be where I am. You know the way to the place where I am going."

5 - Thomas said to him, "Lord, we don't know where you are going, so how can we know the way?"

6 - Jesus answered, "I am the way the truth and the life. No one comes to the Father except through me."

7 - "If you really knew me, you would know my Father as well. From now on, you do know him and have seen him."

8 - Philip said, "Lord, show us the Father and that will be enough for us."

9 - Jesus answered: "Don't you know me, Philip, even after I have been among you such a long time? Anyone who has seen me has seen the Father. How can you say, 'Show us the Father'?"

10 - "Don't you believe that I am in the Father and the Father is in me? The words I say to you are not just my own. Rather, it is the Father, living in me, who is doing the work."

11 - "Believe me when I say that I am in the Father and the Father is in me; or at least believe me on the evidence of the miracles themselves."

12 - "I tell you the truth, anyone who has faith in me will do what I have been doing. He will do even greater things than these, because I am going to the Father."

13-14 - "And I will do whatever you ask in my name, so that the Son may bring glory to the Father. You may ask me for anything in my name, and I will do it."

Bible Facts

Books of the Bible

1. **What is the Bible?** The Bible is the Word of God written by men who were inspired by the Holy Spirit. It is my unfailing guide to right living and to eternal life.

2. **How many books are in the Old Testament? In the New Testament? In the Old and New Testament together?** There are 39 books in the Old Testament, 27 in the New Testament, and 66 altogether.

3. **What are the five types of Books in the Old Testament?** Law, History, Poetry, Major Prophets, Minor Prophets.

4. **Name the Books of Law**. Genesis, Exodus, Leviticus, Numbers, Deuteronomy.

5. **Name the Books of History**. Joshua, Judges, Ruth, 1st and 2nd Samuel, 1st and 2nd Kings, 1st and 2nd Chronicles, Ezra, Nehemiah, Esther.

6. **Name the Books of Poetry**. Job, Psalms, Proverbs, Ecclesiastes, Song of Solomon.

7. **Name the Books of the Major Prophets**. Isaiah, Jeremiah, Lamentations, Ezekiel, Daniel.

8. **Name the Books of the Minor Prophets**. Hosea, Joel, Amos, Obadiah, Jonah, Micah, Nahum, Habakkuk, Zephaniah, Haggai, Zechariah, Malachi.

9. **What are the five types of Books in the New Testament?** Gospel, History, Letters of Paul, Letters of Other Apostles, Prophecy.

10. **Name the Books of the Gospel and the one Book of History.** Matthew, Mark, Luke, John and Acts.

11. **Name the letters of the Apostle Paul.** Romans, 1st and 2nd Corinthians, Galatians, Ephesians, Philippians, Colossians, 1st and 2nd Thessalonians, 1st and 2nd Timothy, Titus, Philemon.

12. **Name the letters of the other Apostles**. Hebrews, James, 1st and 2nd Peter, 1st, 2nd and 3rd John, Jude.

13. **Name the one Book of Prophecy**. Revelation.

14. **Name all 66 books of the Bible in consecutive order**.

Bible Passages for Study

Genesis 6-9: Noah
Genesis 12:1-8; 18:16-32; 22:1-18 - Abraham
Numbers 13:1-14:38; Joshua 14:6-14 - Caleb
I Samuel 14:1-23 - Jonathan
I Samuel 17:1-58 - David
II Chronicles 20:1-30 - Jehoshophat
The Book of Esther: Esther
Job 1:1-2:10; 19:1-29; 42:1-17 – Job
Daniel 3:1-30 - Three Hebrew Captives
Daniel 6 – who prayed three times a day
Matthew 8:1-4 - The Leper
Matthew 8:5-13 - The Centurion
Matthew 9:18-26 - The Ruler and the Afflicted Woman
Matthew 15:21-28 - The Canaanite Woman
Mark 10:46-52 - Blind Bartimaus
I Kings 17-21 - Elijah: Man of Faith; A Man Like Us
II Kings 2:1-12 - Elisha
John 1:1-34 - Sonship by Faith
John 3:1-21 - Everlasting Life by Faith
John 6:1-40 - Abundant Life by Faith
John 9:1-41 - Understanding (or light) by Faith
John 11:1-44 - Resurrection by Faith
John 14:1-3 - Heaven by Faith
John 14:12 - Mighty Works by Faith
Matthew 14:22-23 - Peter Walks on Water

Matthew 8:10 - When Jesus heard this, he was astonished and said to those following him, "I tell you the truth, I have not found anyone in Israel with such **great faith**.

Matthew 9:29 - Then he touched their eyes and said, **"According to your faith will it be done to you."**

Matthew 17:20 - He replied, "Because you have so little faith. I tell you the truth, **if you have faith** as small as a mustard seed, you can say to this mountain, 'Move from here to there' and it will move. Nothing will be impossible for you."

Matthew 21:21 - Jesus replied, "I tell you the truth, **if you have faith and do not doubt**, not only can you do what was done to the fig tree, but also you can say to this mountain, 'Go, throw yourself into the sea,' and it will be done.

Luke 17:5 - The apostles said to the Lord, "**Increase our faith!"**

John 14:12 - I tell you the truth, **anyone who has faith in me** will do what I have been doing. He will do even greater things than these, because I am going to the Father.

Acts 26:18 - to open their eyes and turn them from darkness to light, and from the power of Satan to God, so that they may receive forgiveness of sins and a place among those who are **sanctified by faith in me.**'

Romans 5:1 - Therefore, since **we have been justified through faith**, we have peace with God through our Lord Jesus Christ.

Romans 10:17 - Consequently, **faith comes from hearing the message**, and the message is heard through the word of Christ.

1 Corinthians 16:13 - Be on your guard; **stand firm in the faith**; be men of courage; be strong.

Ephesians 6:16 - In addition to all this, take up the **shield of faith**, with which you can extinguish all the flaming arrows of the evil one.

Hebrews 11:6 - And **without faith it is impossible to please God**, because anyone who comes to him must **believe** that he exists and that he rewards those who earnestly seek him.

Hebrews 11:1, 39 - By faith...these were **all commended for their faith**, yet none of them received what had been promised.

James 1:3 - because you know that the testing of your faith develops perseverance.

James 2:20 - You foolish man, do you want evidence that **faith without deeds is useless?**

Romans 10:9 - That if you confess with your mouth, "Jesus is Lord**," and believe in your heart** that God raised him from the dead, you will be saved.

1 John 5:14 - **This is the confidence we have** in approaching God: that if we ask anything according to his will, he hears us.

1 Corinthians 16:13 - Be on your guard; **stand firm in the faith**; be men of **courage**; be strong.

Psalm 42:11 - Why are you downcast, O my soul? Why so disturbed within me? **Put your hope in God**, for I will yet praise him, my Savior and my God.

Psalm 119:74 - May those who fear you rejoice when they see me, for I have put **my hope in your word**.

Romans 5:3-4 - Not only so, but we also rejoice in our sufferings, because we know that suffering produces perseverance; perseverance, character; and character, **hope**.

Hebrews 12:1 - Therefore, since we are surrounded by such a great cloud of witnesses, let us throw off everything that hinders and the sin that so easily entangles, and **let us run with perseverance** the race marked out for us.

James 1:3 - You know that the testing of your **faith** develops **perseverance.**

Psalm 56:11 - **In God I trust**; I will not be afraid. What can man do to me?

Psalm 143:8 - Let the morning bring me word of your unfailing love, for **I have put my trust in you**. Show me the way I should go, for to you I lift up my soul.

Proverbs 3:5 - **Trust in the LORD with all your heart** and lean not on your own understanding.

Projects and Activities

1. *Faith* - Use hand motions or visuals with memory work to help the child understand Faith, which is "seeing with my heart," not only reading words.

2. ✝ A good dinner table quiz is learning to name the Books of the Bible. One way to do this is to play "concentration."

3. *Purposefulness/Self-Confidence* - Have each individual child sit in on a session with Dad and Mom as they discuss goal setting. Have a classroom-taught child sit in on parent-teacher conference where goals are set. Use the model in this book if you need to. Example: A long term goal could be to read through the entire Bible.

4. *Faith* - Read together the book, *Is That Really You, God?* by Loren Cunningham. *from YWAM Publishing,* (See Resources)

5. *Faith* - Keep a diary, or a prayer journal to help children see prayers answered: some short term, some long term, some He answers, "no." Children need to learn how to pray and that:
    - God delights in answering specific needs and prayers
    - He desires to hear our hearts, not just a “shopping list” of wants
    - He lives and abides in our worship and praise
    - He hears the prayers of the righteous
    - When we honor Him, he will honor us
    - We can use the name and authority of Jesus
    - As we learn His will, our prayers and desires will become more like His
    - We are to pray without ceasing, keep asking
    - Some prayers take time to receive answers
    - God uses creative and unexpected ways to answer our prayers
    - God wants us to have an attitude of prayer – talk to Him all the time
    - Nothing is too big or small for God to care and answer: “Help me stop biting my nails.” “Show me what to do with my life.” “Release the missionaries being held by terrorists.”

6. *Faith/Optimism* - Discuss how "unanswered prayers" (when God says “no”) help us to see God's perspective.

8. When studying that faith can move mountains, use a bulletin board with a mountain, having each child's problem or request on it. As the answers come, move the mountain.

9. *Faith* - Add a dry bean to a jar each time you have, or hear of, an answered prayer.

10. *Faith* - Study characters in the Bible or history who demonstrate Faith.

11. *Faith/Security* - Keep a Faith Scrapbook. Have friends and relatives visit the family to share answered prayer or God's intervention. Follow up by using a page in the scrapbook to record or document each story.

12. *Faith/Security* - Make a Picture Prayer Book using pictures of everyone you want to pray for regularly. You can include picture taking as part of the Project. Write letters to ask for snapshots from those far away. Use the book to teach intercession by "praying through" the book each day.

13. *Faith/Purposefulness/Optimism* - Study the Mayflower Separatists, their pastor, and the great faith of their congregation. Of special interest is Pastor Robinson's farewell prayer. A good source is the account of the Plymouth Settlement in *Plymouth Plantation Classics*, Mantle Ministries (See Resources).

14. *Faith/Purposefulness/Courage* - Study the revival of The Great Awakening of America and England. Many great preachers and evangelists were from this era.

15. *Faith/Security* - Discuss fearful times in the night (the opposite of Faith) – bad dreams, the dark, etc. and read Psalm 3:3-5, 8. Then discuss how (and why) calling on Jesus, out loud, quiets the soul, brings the Holy Spirit to protect. Explain that the darkness or cause of the fear has no place because Jesus is light and peace.

16. *Belief/Optimism* - Study together *Prayer of Jabez*, Bruce Wilkinson's, from Multomah Publishers (See Resources).

17. *Faith/Belief* - Study Jesus' miracles. Discuss how He never refused or denied a healing because He came to restore and bring life.

Reminder: There are general suggestions for Projects and Activities listed on Page 125 that may apply to this Unit Study.

Fear of the Lord

Key Verses

FEAR OF THE LORD - The eyes of the Lord are everywhere, keeping watch on the wicked and the good. Proverbs 15:3

AVAILABILITY - For I have no one else like him, who takes a genuine interest in your welfare. For everyone looks out for his own interests, not those of Jesus Christ. Philippians 2:20-21

BOLDNESS - Now, Lord, consider their threats and enable Your servants to speak your Word with great boldness. Acts 4:29

DELIBERATION - I turned my mind to understand, to investigate, and to search out wisdom and the scheme of things and to understand the stupidity of wickedness and the madness of folly. Ecclesiastes 7:25

DETERMINATION - I have fought the good fight, I have finished the race, I have kept the faith. Now there is in store for me the crown of righteousness, which the Lord, the righteous Judge, will award to me on that day. 2 Timothy 4:7, 8

FIRMNESS - Therefore, my dear brothers, stand firm. Let nothing move you. Always give yourselves fully to the work of the Lord, because you know that your labor in the Lord is not in vain. 1 Corinthians 16:13

GRATEFULNESS - And what do you have that you did not receive? And if you did receive it, why do you boast as if you did not? 1 Corinthians 4:7

HUMILITY - But He gives us more grace. That is why Scripture says, 'God opposes the proud but gives grace to the humble'. James 4:6

Definitions

FEAR OF THE LORD is remembering that God watches my every thought, word, and deed, and that He loves me too much not to correct me for wrong.

AVAILABILITY is being open and willing to meet needs wherever I am needed and rejecting ambitions that hinder me from meeting those needs. *Having the power to produce effect.*

BOLDNESS is being quick to speak or act at the right time, because I am confident that my words and deeds are important. *Courage, bravery, fearlessness.*

DELIBERATION is carefully examining the choices before making a decision. *The act of weighing and examining the reasons for and against a choice or measure.*

DETERMINATION is expending whatever energy is necessary to complete a project. *Decision of a question in the mind; settled purpose.*

FIRMNESS is persisting to base my attitudes and actions on what I know God has purposed, regardless of opposition or discouragement. *Stability; strength; steadfastness; constancy; fixedness.*

GRATEFULNESS is making known to God and others in what ways they have benefited my life. *Being kindly disposed towards one from whom a favor has been received.*

HUMILITY is recognizing the true extent to which God and others are responsible for my successes

RESPECT FOR AUTHORITY - Obey your leaders and submit to their authority. They keep watch over you as men who must give account. Hebrews 13:17

RESPECT FOR AUTHORITY is acting and speaking in a way that demonstrates my honor the special people God has put in charge of me. *To view or consider with some degree of reverence.*

REVERENCE - Therefore, since we are receiving a kingdom that cannot be shaken, let us be thankful, and so worship God acceptably, with reverence and awe. Hebrews 12:28

REVERENCE is giving proper honor to people in positions of authority. *Expressing veneration or submission.*

STANDING AGAINST PEER PRESSURE - Put on the full armor of God so that you can take your stand against the devil's schemes. Ephesians 6:11

STANDING AGAINST PEER PRESSURE is making choices based on the issue rather than on what my friends want me to choose.

YIELDING OF RIGHTS - I urge you, brothers, in view of God's mercy, to offer your bodies as living sacrifices, holy and pleasing to God - this is your spiritual act of worship. Romans 12:1

YIELDING OF RIGHTS is giving up what I could demand in order to fit in with God's plans for me.

Hymn

O Worship the King

O worship the King, all glorious above,
And gratefully sing His pow'r and His love;
Our Shield and Defender, the Ancient of Days,
Pavilioned in splendor and girded with praise.

O tell of His might, O sing of His grace,
Whose robe is the light, whose canopy space.
His chariots of wrath the deep thunderclouds form,
And dark is His path on the wings of the storm.

Thy bountiful care what tongue can recite?
It breathes in the air, it shines in the light;
It streams from the hills, it descends to the plain,
And sweetly distills in the dew and the rain.

Frail children of dust, and feeble as frail,
In Thee do we trust, nor find Thee to fail;
Thy mercies, how tender! How firm to the end!
Our Maker, Defender, Redeemer and Friend.
Thy bountiful care what tongue can recite?
It breathes in the air, it shines in the light;
It streams from the hills, it descends to the plain,
And sweetly distills in the dew and the rain.

Frail children of dust, and feeble as frail,
In Thee do we trust, nor find Thee to fail;
Thy mercies, how tender! How firm to the end!
Our Maker, Defender, Redeemer and Friend.

Scripture for Memorization and Meditation

Psalm 139

1-3 - O Lord, you have searched me and you know me. You know when I sit and when I rise; you perceive my thoughts from afar. You discern my going out and my lying down; you are familiar with all my ways.

4-6 - Before a word is on my tongue you know it completely, O Lord. You hem me in _ behind and before; you have laid your hand upon me. Such knowledge is too wonderful for me, too lofty for me to attain.

7-10 - Where can I go from your Spirit? Where can I flee from your presence? If I go up to the heavens, you are there; if I make my bed in the depths, you are there. If I rise on the wings of the dawn, if I settle on the far side of the sea, even there your hand will guide me, your right hand will hold me fast.

11-12 - If I say, "Surely the darkness will hide me and the light become night around me," even the darkness will not be dark to you; the night will shine like the day, for darkness is as light to you.

13-14 - For you created my inmost being; you knit me together in my mother's womb. I praise you because I am fearfully and wonderfully made; your works are wonderful, I know that full well.

15-16 - My frame was not hidden from you when I was made in the secret place. When I was woven together in the depths of the earth, your eyes saw my unformed body. All the days ordained for me were written in your book before one of them came to be.

17-18 - How precious to me are your thoughts, O God! How vast is the sum of them! Were I to count them, they would out number the grains of sand. When I awake I am still with you.

23-24 - Search me, O God, and know my heart; test me and know my anxious thoughts. See if there is any offensive way in me, and lead me in the way everlasting.

Bible Facts

The Creation

1. **What book and chapters of the Bible tell about the creation of heaven and earth?** Genesis 1 and 2 tell about the creation of heaven and earth.

2. **In how many days did God create heaven and earth and all the things in them?** God created all things in six days.

3. **What did God do on the first day of creation?** On the first day, God created light and separated it from darkness.

4. **What did God do on the second day of creation?** On the second day, God created the firmament and divided the waters above and below it.

5. **What did God do on the third day of creation?** On the third day, God created plants and trees.

6. **What did God do on the fourth day of creation?** On the fourth day, God created the sun, moon, and stars.

7. **What did God do on the fifth day of creation?** On the fifth day, God created birds and sea animals.

8. **What did God do on the sixth day of creation?** On the sixth day, God created animals that move on the land, and He created man.

9. **Having completed His creation, what did God do on the seventh day?** On the seventh day, God rested and made it a holy day.

10. **How did God create the first man?** God formed Adam, the first man, from the dust of the ground and breathed into him the breath of life.

11. **How did God create the first woman?** God made Eve, the first woman, from the rib of the side of Adam.

12. **What is so special about God's creation of man and woman?** Of all the creation, only man and woman were made in God's own image.

Bible Passages for Study

Genesis 3:1-19 - Adam and Eve's sin
Genesis 4 - Am I my brother's keeper?
Genesis 22:12 - Abraham
Genesis 28:16, 17; 43:18 - Jacob
Exodus 1:17, 21 - Hebrew Children
Deuteronomy 10:12, 31:12 - God's requirement
Joshua 4:24 - God is mighty
1 Samuel 11:7 - Saul's victory
1 Kings 18 - Elijah and the Prophets of Baal
1 Kings 18:3, 4 - Obadiah
2 Chronicles 14:14; 19:9; 26:5
2 Chronicles 20:3 - Jehoshaphat
Nehemiah 5:15 - Nehemiah
Job 28:28
Job 38 - 42 God's power & authority in creation
Jeremiah 26:19 - Hezekiah
Daniel 1-3 - The Three Hebrews
The Book of Jonah
Haggai 1:5 - Levi
Haggai 1:12 - Jews
Acts 5:5-11 - Ananias and Sapphira
Acts 9:31 - Fear of the Lord and rest
Acts 10:2 - Cornelius
Acts 19:17 - Results of Fear of the Lord in believers
2 Corinthians 7:11 - Results in repentance
Hebrews 11:7 - Noah
Hebrews 12:28 - Reverence and Godly fear

Projects and Activities

1. ✝ *Fear of the Lord/Reverence* - Study the awesomeness of God. Nature walks can demonstrate His awesomeness. Talk about how we often compare God with our earthly father. Point out that God is perfect, although our earthly fathers are imperfect.

2. ✝ Study astronomy from a creationist's viewpoint

3. *Fear of the Lord* - Study scriptures on creation outside of the book of Genesis. Use a concordance or topical index looking up words such as: stars, heavens, the deep, formed, wonders, etc. Job and Psalms are both filled with passages.

4. ✝ Study Psalm 139 and discuss our Creator God with the emphasis on "God watches me." Prepare a pantomime presentation based on the Psalm, acting out the verses. If you have someone who could teach some of the sign language, this could be intertwined with the movement depicting this Psalm.

5. *Gratefulness/Reverence* - Study the early verses in Proverbs which refer to God's awesomeness.

6. *Fear of the Lord* - Study The Trinity: The Father, the Son, and the Holy Spirit.

7. *Reverence/Gratefulness/Humility* - One father was dealing with a son who wanted to do things his own way. One Saturday the father took him out in a boat, a distance away from land. Then the father went down for a nap, telling the boy to get the boat back to land. After much time the boy came to the dad asking for help. Afterwards, he was a changed boy. The dad trusted that God would get the lesson home that "we need each other." Similar lessons could be learned in the kitchen, laundry room, on camping trips, etc.

8. *Faith* - Study the importance of prayer. Ask, "How do we pray?" "What is the purpose of prayer?" Write a puppet story of a little girl praying. The girl hears God's voice but doesn't recognize it as God; Or use the story of Samuel and Eli.

9. *Humility/Reverence* -Discuss the meaning of "respect". How do we show respect for God? For others? What is expected of us during times of family or congregational worship or learning? How can we gain the most from these times of "gathering together"?

10. *Humility/Reverence* Write a letter to God.

11. ✝ An art Project can show God's wonderful creation. Have children draw pictures of themselves, showing their own uniqueness. Then they can make a collage of pictures of their friends.

12. ✝ One group did a Unit Study on the physical qualities of light and darkness. They researched how Scripture treats light and dark: God created light; dark is its absence.

13. *Fear of the Lord* - One group studied Psalm 139:12 and discussed the world's view that "if no one sees it, it's ok; if I don't get caught, then no one knows and it's ok." This moral lesson could be tied in with a study of science.

14. *Fear of the Lord* - Study the difference between the *Fear of Man* and the *Fear of God*. What is the right kind of fear? Realizing God is the One with Whom we have to deal, we don't need to fear man. Charles Finney said, "What would you need to change the world? A handful of men who feared nothing but God and hated nothing but sin."

15. *Fear of the Lord* - Study Bible Stories about how the *Fear of Man* can lead one astray: such as Saul's sacrifice because of the pressure of the people when Samuel was delayed; Aaron who built the calf; Abraham who lied to Pharaoh about Sarah being his wife; Moses hitting the rock instead of speaking to it because of the people's anger. Have the children identify other Scriptures.

16. *Fear of the Lord* - Study Bible Stories about how the *Fear of God* can overcome the Fear of Man: Daniel; three men in fiery furnace; Elijah, Josiah and Paul.

17. *Reverence* - Paint a "designer shirt" of handprints demonstrating how God made us each unique. Read Colossians 3:9-17 in the message translation regarding the "Custom made by the Creator" label.

18. ✝ Create a special prayer journal with each child. This could take the place of a diary. It could include the child's own prayers, special verses, creative writing exercises, memories of special trips and important events.

19. *Reverence* - Use materials from Creation Science Institute. Discuss the scientific evidence in relation to the Scriptures.

20. *Fear of the Lord* - Study the different names of God and how we can respond to them.

21. *Fear of the Lord* - Research the meanings of the words: omniscient, omnipresent, omnipotent, etc.

22. *Standing Against Peer Pressure* - Discuss the principle of: standing alone. Discuss how this requires the sub-qualities of this unit. *Before* situations come up, practice how we should respond when asked to go along with friends with wrong choices. Be prepared with determined and firm answers.

23. ✝ Study the development of a baby in the womb (from scripture memory of Psalm 139:13-16). Find a relative or church friend who is expecting and ask her to let your family be a part of those months.

24. *Humility/Reverence* - Visit the highest place in your area where you can see 360 degrees around you. Read together Psalm 139:7-10 where it says, "Is there any place that God cannot see?" How far can you see?

25. *Humility* - Make a room in your house represent your "heart." After dark hide some things in it and find them with a flashlight. Memorize Psalm 139: 23-24.

26. *Humility* - Put together a three dimensional puzzle or build a model of the human body. Discuss how God our Creator and Master Designer wove every intricate part of what makes me Me.

27. *Determination* - Play a game of concentration, requiring focused attention. Who is the best?

Reminder: There are general suggestions for Projects and Activities listed on Page 125 that may apply to this Unit Study.

Integrity

Key Verses

INTEGRITY - The man of integrity walks securely, but he who takes crooked paths will be found out. Proverbs 10:9

ALERTNESS - Watch and pray so that you will not fall into temptation. The spirit is willing, but the body is weak. Mark 14:38

DEPENDABILITY - Who may dwell in your sanctuary? Who keeps his oath even when it hurts.
Psalm 15:1, 4

DISCIPLINE - Like a city whose walls are broken down is a man who lacks self-control. Proverbs 25:28

ENDURANCE - Let us not become weary in doing good, for at the proper time we will reap a harvest if we do not give up.
Galatians 6:9

LEADERSHIP - But the wisdom that comes from heaven is first of all pure; then peace-loving, considerate, submissive, full of mercy and good fruit, impartial and sincere.
James 3:17

Definitions

INTEGRITY is honesty in all parts of my life; it is doing the things I say others ought to do or "practicing what I preach."

ALERTNESS is the ability to anticipate right responses to that which is taking place around me. *Watchful, active in vigilance.*

DEPENDABILITY is doing what I said I would, even if I learn afterwards that it would be unpleasant; fulfilling what I agree to do even though it requires unexpected sacrifices. *Able to be depended upon.*

DISCIPLINE is submitting to the training process which is demanded by Christ's Lordship to produce order in every aspect of my life. *Education; instruction; cultivation and improvement; subjection to laws, rules, order; correction; chastisement.*

ENDURANCE is not giving up on the goals God and I have, instead, continuing in faith when I am discouraged or when others want me to quit. *Continuing under pain or distress without resistance, or without sinking or yielding to the pressure.*

LEADERSHIP is the willingness to be an example and organizer of others to accomplish a goal. *Showing the way by going first.*

MATURITY – Let us leave the elementary teachings about Christ and go on to maturity. Hebrews 6:1

MATURITY is development mentally, socially, physically and spiritually that's appropriate for me.*Completeness of age or judgment.*

PERSUASIVENESS - And the Lord's servant must not quarrel; instead, he must be kind to everyone, able to teach, not resentful. II Timothy 2:24

PURSUASIVENESS is being able to influence others by use of sound reasoning. *Having influence on the mind or passion.*

SELF-ACCEPTANCE - This is what the Lord says - He Who made you, Who formed you in the womb, and Who will help you; "Do not be afraid...I have chosen you." Isaiah 44:2

SELF-ACCEPTANCE is accepting the way I am because I know God is working in my life for my highest good.

TRUSTWORTHINESS - Since an overseer is entrusted with God's work, he must be blameless. Titus 1:7

TRUSTWORTHINESS is earning the respect of others by my attitudes and actions. *It is the quality by which a person deserves the confidence of others.*

TRUTHFULNESS - The Lord detests lying lips, but He delights in men who are truthful. Proverbs 12:22

TRUTHFULNESS is telling the facts in every situation regardless of the consequences.

Hymn

Living for Jesus

Living for Jesus, a life that is true,
Striving to please Him in all that I do;
Yielding allegiance, gladhearted and free;
This is the pathway of blessing for me.

Living for Jesus who died in my place,
Bearing on Calv'ry my sin and disgrace;
Such love constrains me to answer His call;
Follow His leading and give Him my all.

Living for Jesus wherever I am,
Doing each duty in His holy Name;
Willing to suffer affliction and loss,
Deeming each trial a part of my cross.

~ Chorus ~

O Jesus, Lord and Savior, I give myself to Thee,
For Thou in Thine atonement didst give Thyself for me.
I own no other master, my heart shall be Thy throne;
My life I give, henceforth to live, O Christ, for Thee alone!

Scripture for Memorization and Meditation

Selected Proverbs

3:9-10 - Honor the Lord with your wealth, with the firstfruits of all your crops; then your barns will be filled to overflowing, and your vats will brim over with new wine.

20:22 - Do not say, "I'll pay you back for this wrong!" Wait for the Lord, and he will deliver you.

11:12 - A man who lacks judgment derides his neighbor, but a man of understanding holds his tongue.

15:1 - A gentle answer turns away wrath, but a harsh word stirs up anger.

3:27 - Do not withhold good from those who deserve it, when it is in your power to act.

14:23 - All hard work brings a profit, but mere talk leads only to poverty.

Bible Facts

Old Testament Prophecies of Christ

1. **Where is the prophecy recorded that Jesus would be born of a virgin?** Isaiah 7:14.

2. **Where is the prophecy that Jesus would be born in Bethlehem?** Micah 5:2

3. **Where is the prophecy that Jesus would teach in parables?** Psalm 78:2

4. **Where is the prophecy that Jesus would come as a king riding on a donkey?** Zechariah 9:9

5. **Where is the prophecy that Jesus would be betrayed for 30 pieces of silver?** Zechariah 11:12-13

6. **Where is the prophecy that not a bone of Jesus' body would be broken?** Psalm 34:20

7. **Where is the prophecy that Jesus would be raised from the grave?** Psalm 16:9-10

8. **What two prophetic chapters in the Old Testament tell most completely about Jesus' suffering and death?** Psalm 22 and Isaiah 53

9. **Name five important facts about Jesus' suffering prophesied in Psalm 22.**
   He felt forsaken by God.
   He was mocked by the onlookers.
   His hands and feet were pierced.
   His bones were out of joint.
   His garments were divided by casting lots.

10. **Name five important facts about Jesus' suffering prophesied in Isaiah 53.**
   He did not even open His mouth before his accusers.
   He was despised and rejected by men.
   By His wounds we are healed.
   The Lord laid our sins on Him.
   He was buried in a rich man's grave.

Bible Passages for Study

Genesis 1-3 - Creation, the Fall
Exodus 1-2 - Miriam
Deuteronomy 9:5 - Cleansing the Promised Land
1 Samuel 3 - Samuel
1 Samuel 17 - David
1 Kings 9:4 - Solomon
1 Chronicles 15:22 - Skillful Musician
Joshua 1 - Joshua
Nehemiah 7:2 - Hananiah
Job 2:9 - Job and His Wife
Psalm 25:21; 41:12; 78:72
Proverbs 10:9; 13:6; 29:10
Matthew 22:16 - The Pharisees' Lack of Integrity
Matthew 25:1-13 - The Ten Virgins
Acts 6:3 - The First Deacons
Acts 18:6 - Paul's Integrity
Titus 2:7 - A Good Pastor
Luke 19:2-10 - The Story of Zacchaeus
Luke 15:1-7 - Parable of the Lost Lamb
Matthew 25:14-30 - Parable of the Talents

1 Kings 9:4 "As for you, **if you walk before me in integrity of heart** and uprightness, as David your father did, and do all I command and observe my decrees and laws,

Job 2:3 then the LORD said to Satan, "Have you considered my servant Job? there is no one on earth like him; he is blameless and upright, a man who fears God and shuns evil. And he still maintains his **integrity**, though you incited me against him to ruin him without any reason."

Psalms 7:8 let the LORD judge the peoples. Judge me, O LORD, according to my righteousness, according to my **integrity**, O Most High.

Proverbs 11:3 **the integrity of the upright guides them**, but the unfaithful are destroyed by their duplicity.

Proverbs 13:6 **Righteousness guards the man of integrity**, but wickedness overthrows the sinner.

Titus 2:7 In everything set them an example by doing what is good. In your teaching show **integrity**, seriousness

Ephesians 6:18 And pray in the Spirit on all occasions with all kinds of prayers and requests. With this in mind, **be alert** and always keep on praying for all the saints.

1 Thessalonians 5:6 So then, let us not be like others, who are asleep, but let us **be alert** and self-controlled.

1 Peter 5:8 Be self-controlled and **alert**. Your enemy the devil prowls around like a roaring lion looking for someone to devour.

Deuteronomy 21:18 If a man has a stubborn and rebellious son who does not obey his father and mother and will not listen to them when they **discipline** him,

Psalms 94:12 **Blessed is the man you discipline**, O LORD, the man you teach from your law;

Proverbs 1:7 The fear of the LORD is the beginning of knowledge, **but fools despise wisdom and discipline.**

Proverbs 3:11 My son, **do not despise the Lord's discipline** and do not resent his rebuke,

Proverbs 6:23 For these commands are a lamp, this teaching is a light, and the **corrections of discipline are the way to life**,

Proverbs 12:1 **Whoever loves discipline loves knowledge**, but he who hates correction is stupid.

Proverbs 13:24 He who spares the rod hates his son, **but he who loves him is careful to discipline him.**

Proverbs 15:5 A fool spurns his father's discipline, but **whoever heeds correction shows prudence.**

Proverbs 22:15 Folly is bound up in the heart of a child, but the **rod of discipline will drive it far from him**.

2 Timothy 1:7 For God did not give us a spirit of timidity, but a spirit of power, of love and of **self-discipline**.

Hebrews 12:7 **Endure hardship as discipline**; God is treating you as sons. For what son is not disciplined by his father?

Hebrews 12:8 **If you are not disciplined** and everyone undergoes discipline), then you are illegitimate children and not true sons.

Hebrews 12:11 **No discipline seems pleasant at the time**, but painful. Later on, however, it produces a harvest of righteousness and peace for those who have been trained by it.

Romans 15:5 May the **God who gives endurance** and encouragement give you a spirit of unity among yourselves as you follow Christ Jesus,

1 Thessalonians 1:3 We continually remember before our God and Father your work produced by faith, your labor prompted by love, and **your endurance inspired by hope** in our Lord Jesus Christ.

Hebrews 6:1 therefore let us leave the elementary teachings about Christ and go on to **maturity**, not laying again the foundation of repentance from acts that lead to death, and of faith in God,

1 Corinthians 2:4 My message and my preaching were not with wise and **persuasive** words, but with a demonstration of the Spirit's power,

Proverbs 11:13 A gossip betrays a confidence, but a trustworthy man keeps a secret.

Proverbs 13:17 A wicked messenger falls into trouble, **but a trustworthy envoy brings healing**.

Luke 19:17 "'Well done, my good servant!' his master replied. 'Because you have been **trustworthy** in a very small matter, take charge of ten cities.'

Projects and Activities

1. ✝ Study together the book of Proverbs. As you read it, list Character Qualities and the references.
2. *Integrity/Discipline* - Discuss the *Ten Basic Steps of Discipline* from 23 during this study.
3. *Integrity* - Study the biography of a person from history, such as a godly general, a president, an inventor, or an athlete, who showed one of the Sub-Qualities.
4. ✝ Have each child write a story whose main character demonstrates one of the Sub-Qualities.
5. *Maturity* - Write a speech telling the consequences of drug or alcohol use.
6. *Pursuasiveness* - Have the children debate a current world issue with one playing "the devil's advocate."
7. *Self-Acceptance* - View a video together of a person who has struggled to overcome a handicap, then discuss self-acceptance. Ideas: *My Left Foot*; *Chariots of Fire*.
8. *Maturity* - Discuss and list the differences between chronological age and the characteristics of a mature person.
9. *Truthfulness* - Write and perform a skit showing the types of situations where a child might face the need to choose truthfulness.
10. *Discipline/Trustworthiness* - For one week, keep track of how the child is able to obey the first time without delay; or do a chore without being reminded, etc.
11. *Endurance/Self-Discipline* - Assign a task to the child that you know will take time, endurance, and self-discipline. Have the project take several days to complete. It could be at home, at church, in the community.
12. *Leadership, Alertness, Truthfulness, Integrity* - Give the child opportunities for a week to be an arbitrator between siblings, friends, or to be the problem solver over family issues. Have him focus on the responsibilities of leadership, alertness, truthfulness, integrity, and cooperation.
13. *Integrity* - Look through editorials of the newspaper for one week, looking for those that spotlight integrity versus those expressing contentiousness or selfish opinion.
14. *Discipline/Endurance/Dependability* – This is a great unit to combine with introducing a new sport. Track and field or cross country work especially well for learning these qualities.

15. *Integrity* – Before a special social gathering, such as a slumber party, field trip, church pot-luck, etc., have a lesson on how we can both look for qualities in this unit in others, and how we can exemplify them in our own actions. Use the event to look for these in others and try to practice them.

16. *Integrity/Maturity* - Ask each person to think of a teen or young adult they know who demonstrates the most of the Unit's Qualities. Why were they chosen? What shows their maturity and integrity?

17. *Integrity* – Older children may be able to understand the principle of *Self-Government*. A few good teachings on this topic are available through home schooling suppliers. Its principles are basically "knowing your place in God and with people," "governing yourself with a life of integrity," and "being above reproach."

18. *Integrity/Alertness/Trustworthiness/Maturity* - For older children, have a lesson on choosing right friends and evaluating one's own true character.

Reminder: There are general suggestions for Projects and Activities listed on Page 125 that may apply to this Unit Study.

Joy

Key Verses

JOY - This day is sacred to our Lord. Do not grieve, for the joy of the Lord is your strength. Nehemiah 8:10

APPRECIATIVE - Praise the Lord, O my soul, and forget not all his benefits. Psalm 103:2

CHEERFULNESS - A cheerful look brings joy to the heart, and good news gives health to the bones. Proverbs 15:30

CONTENTMENT - And if we have food and covering, with these we shall be content. 1 Timothy 6:8

CREATIVITY - Do not conform any longer to the pattern of this world, but be transformed by the renewing of your mind. Then you will be able to test and approve what God's will is - His good, pleasing, and perfect will. Romans 12:2

ENTHUSIASM – A cheerful look brings joy to the heart, and good news gives health to the bones. Proverbs 15:30

HUMOR - A happy heart makes the face cheerful, but heartache crushes the spirit. Proverbs 15:13

THANKFULNESS - Give thanks in all circumstances, for this is God's will for you in Christ Jesus. 1 Thessalonians 5:18

Definitions

JOY is choosing to have a glad heart in every circumstance of life.

APPRECIATIVENESS is revealing how another's inward character has brought personal benefit to my life. *To recognize value.*

CHEERFULNESS is assisting others to see the benefit in a difficult situation by my encouraging words and bright countenance. *Life, animation, a state of moderate joy or gaiety.*

CONTENTMENT is remembering that God and those in charge of me have provided everything I need for my present happiness. *Satisfaction of mind with any condition or event.*

CREATIVITY is viewing a need or a task from a new perspective. *Having the ability to bring into being from nothing.*

ENTHUSIASM is encouraging others in their work by my excitement over the reward each task has in itself. *(From a root, meaning 'divinely inspired')*

HUMOR is choosing to see the good or pleasant side of a situation. *Temporary turn of mind or disposition.*

THANKFULNESS is telling God and others how they have benefited me. *Impressed with a sense of that received and ready to acknowledge* it.

Hymn

O for a Thousand Tongues to Sing

O for a thousand tongues to sing
My great Redeemer's praise,
The glories of my God and King,
The triumphs of His grace.

Jesus! The Name that charms our fears,
That bids our sorrows cease,
'Tis music in the sinners' ears,
'Tis life and health and peace.

He breaks the power of canceled sin,
He sets the prisoner free;
His blood can make the foulest clean;
His blood avails for me.

Hear Him, ye deaf; His praise, ye dumb,
Your loosened tongues employ;
Ye blind, behold your Savior come;
And leap, ye lame, for joy.

Bible Facts

The Fruits of the Spirit

1. **Where do we find the listing in Scripture of the Fruits of the Holy Spirit?** In the book of Galatians, Chapter 5, verses 22 and 23.
2. **Name the Fruits of the Spirit.** Love, Joy, Peace, Patience, Kindness, Goodness, Faithfulness, Gentleness, and Self-Control.
3. **With what does the Apostle Paul compare these things?** The desires of the sinful nature.
4. **What does he say will happen to those who live according to the sinful nature?** They will not inherit the kingdom of God.
5. **How does Paul say we can gain the Fruits of the Spirit?** Those who belong to Christ Jesus have crucified the sinful nature with its passions and desires. Since we live by the Spirit, let us keep in step with the Spirit. Galatians 5:24-25.

Scripture for Memorization and Meditation

Philippians 4:4-13

4:4 - Rejoice in the Lord always. I will say it again: Rejoice!

4:5 - Let your gentleness be evident to all. The Lord is near.

4:6 - Do not be anxious about anything, but in everything, by prayer and petition, with thanksgiving, present your requests to God.

4:7 - And the peace of God, which transcends all understanding, will guard your hearts and your minds in Christ Jesus.

4:8 - Finally, brothers, whatever is true, whatever is noble, whatever is right, whatever is pure, whatever is lovely, whatever is admirable--if anything is excellent or praiseworthy--think about such things.

4:9 - Whatever you have learned or received or heard from me, or seen in me--put it into practice. And the God of peace will be with you.

4:10 - I rejoice greatly in the Lord that at last you have renewed your concern for me. Indeed, you have been concerned, but you had no opportunity to show it.

4:11- I am not saying this because I am in need, for I have learned to be content whatever the circumstances.

4:12 - I know what it is to be in need, and I know what it is to have plenty. I have learned the secret of being content in any and every situation, whether well fed or hungry, whether living in plenty or in want.

4:13 - I can do everything through him who gives me strength.

Bible Passages for Study

Deuteronomy 28 – Blessings and Cursings
1 Samuel 18:6 – David
1 Chronicles 15:16 – David's Musicians
2 Chronicles 4-7 – Dedication of the Temple
2 Chronicles 20:27 – Triumphant Celebration
Nehemiah 12:27 – Dedication of the Rebuilt Wall of Jerusalem
Habakkuk 3:18 – Joy Despite Difficulties
Luke 2:1-8 – Jesus' Birth
Luke 15:11-32 – Prodigal Son
Luke 19:37 – Triumphal Entry
Colossians 1:11 – Paul's Prayer
1 Thessalonians 5:16 – Rejoice Evermore

Esther 8:17 In every province and in every city, wherever the edict of the king went, there was **joy** and gladness among the Jews, with feasting and celebrating. And many people of other nationalities became Jews because fear of the Jews had seized them.

Psalms 45:15 They are **led in with joy** and gladness; they enter the palace of the king.

Isaiah 35:10 The ransomed of the LORD will return. They will enter Zion with singing; everlasting **joy will crown their heads**. Gladness and joy will overtake them, and sorrow and sighing will flee away.

Psalms 71:23 **My lips will shout for joy** when I sing praise to you-- I, whom you have redeemed.

Luke 10:21 At that time Jesus, full of **joy through the Holy Spirit**, said, "I praise you, Father, Lord of heaven and earth, because you have hidden these things from the wise and learned, and revealed them to little children. Yes, Father, for this was your good pleasure.

Proverbs 15:13 **A happy heart makes the face cheerful**, but heartache crushes the spirit.

Proverbs 17:22 **A cheerful heart is good medicine**, but a crushed spirit dries up the bones.

2 Corinthians 9:7 Each man should give what he has decided in his heart to give, not reluctantly or under compulsion, for **God loves a cheerful giver**.

Job 36:11 If they obey and serve him, they will spend the rest of their days in prosperity and their years in **contentment**.

1 Timothy 6:6 But **godliness with contentment is great gain**.

Projects and Activities

1. *Joy – Study the idea, "No discipline for the moment seems joyful, but in the end it reaps a harvest of righteousness."* See 1 Peter 4.

1. *Joy* – Make, buy, or print out various happy faces. Cut them out. Find occasion to give as many away as you can in one day or one week.
2. *Creativity* - Discuss why we don't plant flowers where it is already pretty, we plant where it is barren or ugly. Explain the same is needed in peoples' lives. Spread some Joy to others.
3. *Joy* – Visit a newly planted field, return later. Or plant your own vegetable or window garden. Talk about "except a grain of wheat..." And the rebirth which brings Joy. Discuss how we can plant seeds of Joy in others' hearts.
4. *Cheerfulness* - Use drama or art to instill the concept that we need to live the word JOY in our lives: J – esus first, O – thers second; Y – ou last.
5. *Creativity* - Have the children close their eyes and listen to upbeat classical music. Have them picture scenes of Joy, then have an art project portraying what they saw.
6. *Cheerfulness* - Record the group for an hour without their knowledge. Later, ask them to listen for sounds or expressions of Joy or negative emotions such as selfishness, complaining, teasing. It's almost like pictures of themselves.
7. *Joy* - Do skits with the children of situations, first showing negative emotions, then showing joyfulness.
8. *Creativity* - Create a "gadget band" from things that can produce noise: pots and pans, combs, soda bottles, egg beaters, dowels, etc. Use these things to make a joyful noise to the Lord.
9. *Creativity* - Start a tradition of having the family take turns making a centerpiece for the table or a window decoration. Use the imagination for supplies, such as yard or garden items, etc.
10. *Cheerfulness* - Watch the movie *Polyanna* or read the book. Discuss how Polyanna chose to be happy (glad); how she almost gave in to despair. Agree to play the Glad Game for a week, them discuss how it has affected the atmosphere of your home.
11. *Humor* - Begin a humor notebook of cute and humorous comic strips, jokes, and anecdotes.

12. *Creativity* - Start a collection of odd shaped throwaway items, like film canisters and packing peanuts. Have a day to create a 3-D scene of art from your collection.

13. *Creativity* - Create a construction paper playground finding ways to fold, curl, layer, and build up with strips of colored paper. This can be playful and futuristic, or realistic, or abstract. Be creative.

14. *Appreciativeness* - Do a self-imposed *fast* or *lent* of a few of your favorite things. Learn contentment of simpler things in their absence.

15. *Joy/Appreciativeness* - Read the Elsie Dinsmore Book Series and discuss Elsie's joy and appreciativeness.

16. *Creativity* - Create something new: a recipe; a family language, using inside jokes, nicknames, a personal logo; a family logo or *cattle brand*; play money, etc.

17. *Creativity* - Give each person a disposable camera. Have each one create a story from the pictures they take.

18. *Humor* – Begin a notebook of cute and funny things your family members have said and done. Review them when you need to be uplifted.

19. *Joy* - Create a parade of singers and instruments like Nehemiah's wall or David and Solomon had.

22. *Joy* - Make, buy, or print out various happy faces. Find occasions to give as many away as you can in a day or a week.

23. Take an outing to a poor part of town. Imagine what might be missing from the homes you see, and the belongings you have and take for granted. Find ways to give to someone in need that you have seen.

Reminder: There are general suggestions for Projects and Activities listed on Page 125 that may apply to this Unit.

Obedience

Key Verses

OBEDIENCE - Do not merely listen to the Word, and so deceive yourselves. Do what it says. James 1:22

ATTENTIVENESS - We must pay careful attention, therefore, to what we have heard, so that we do not drift away. Hebrews 2:1

COOPERATIVENESS - Make every effort to keep the unity of the Spirit through the bond of peace. Ephesians 4:2

MEEKNESS - Find rest, O my soul, in God alone; my hope comes from Him.
Psalm 62:5

SUBMISSIVENESS - Submit yourselves for the Lord's sake to every authority instituted among men: whether to the king, as the supreme authority, or to governors, who are sent by him to punish those who do wrong and to commend those who do right.
I Peter 2:13

Definitions

OBEDIENCE is promptly and cheerfully doing what I am told by those in charge of me.

ATTENTIVENESS is listening with my eyes, ears and heart. *Heedful, intent, observant, regarding with care.*

COOPERATIVENESS is working together with others for a common purpose. *Operating jointly to the same end.*

MEEKNESS is subduing anger by giving my rights and expectations over to the Lord. *Softness of temper; mildness; gentleness; forbearance under injuries and provocations.*

SUBMISSIVENESS is wanting to hear what others believe is best for me, even if it points out my weaknesses. *Yielding to power or authority.*

Hymn

Trust and Obey

When we walk with the Lord in the light of His Word,
What a glory He sheds on our way!
While we do His good will, He abides with us still,
And with all who will trust and obey.

Not a burden we bear, not a sorrow we share,
But our toil He doth richly repay;
Not a grief or a loss, not a frown or a cross,
But is blest if we trust and obey.

Then in fellowship sweet we will sit at His feet,
Or we'll walk by His side in the way;
What He says we will do, where He sends we will go;
Never fear, only trust and obey.

~ Chorus ~

Trust and obey, for there's no other way
To be happy in Jesus, but to trust and obey.

Bible Facts

1. **To whom did God first give the Ten Commandments?** To the nation of Israel through their leader, Moses.

2. **When did God give Moses these Commandments?** While the Israelites were in the desert near Mount Sinai after they had been set free from Egypt.

3. **Where in the Bible are the Ten Commandments recorded?** In Exodus, chapter 20, and also in Deuteronomy, chapter 5.

4. **Name all Ten commandments in their proper order**.
    1. **You shall have no other gods before me**.
    2. **You shall not make for yourself an idol** in the form of anything in heaven above or on the earth beneath or in the waters below. You shall not bow down to them or worship them; for I, the Lord your God, am a jealous God, punishing the children for the sin of the fathers to the third and fourth generation of those who hate me, but showing love to a thousand generations of those who love me and keep my commandments.
    3. **You shall not misuse the name of the Lord your God**, for the Lord will not hold anyone guiltless who misuses his name.
    4. **Remember the Sabbath day by keeping it holy**. Six days you shall labor and do all your work, but the seventh day is a Sabbath to the Lord your God. On it you shall not do any work, neither you, nor your son or daughter, nor your manservant or maidservant, nor your animals, nor the alien within your gates. For in six days the Lord made the heavens and the earth, the sea, and all that is in them, but he rested on the seventh day. Therefore the Lord blessed the Sabbath day and made it holy.
    5. **Honor your father and your mother**, so that you may live long in the land the Lord your God is giving you.
    6. **You shall not murder**.
    7. **You shall not commit adultery**.
    8. **You shall not give false witness**.
    9. **You shall not steal**.
    10. **You shall not covet** your neighbor's house. You shall not covet your neighbor's wife, or his manservant or maidservant, his ox or donkey, or anything that belongs to your neighbor..

5. **Who are the first four Commandments about?** Our relationship with God.

6. **Who are the last six Commandments about:** Our relationships with one another.

Scripture for Memorization or Meditation

Psalm 19

1-1 - The heavens declare the glory of God; the skies proclaim the work of His hands. Day after day they pour forth speech; night after night they display knowledge.

3-4 - There is no speech or language where their voice is not heard. Their voice goes out into all the earth, their words to the ends of the world.

5-6 - In the heavens he has pitched his tent for the sun, which is like a bridegroom coming forth from his pavilion, like a champion rejoicing to run his course. It rises at one end of the heavens and makes its circuit to the other; nothing is hidden from its heat.

7 - The law of the Lord is perfect, reviving the soul. The statutes of the Lord are trustworthy, making wise the simple.

8 - The precepts of the Lord are right, giving joy to the heart. The commands of the Lord are radiant, giving light to the eyes.

9 - The fear of the Lord is pure, enduring forever. The ordinances of the Lord are sure and altogether righteous.

10-11 - They are more precious than gold, than much fine gold; They are sweeter than honey, than honey from the comb. By them is your servant warned; in keeping them there is great reward.

12-13 - Who can discern his errors? Forgive my hidden faults. Keep your servant also from willful sins; may they not rule over me. Then will I be blameless, innocent of great transgression.

14 - May the words of my mouth and the meditation of my heart be pleasing in your sight, O Lord, my Rock and my Redeemer.

Bible Passages for Study

Genesis 3:1-24 - The Fall
Genesis 6:8-8:1 - Noah
Genesis 12:1-4; 22:1-18 - Abraham
Genesis 20:7 - Abraham's lapse
Exodus 3:11-15; 4:1-5; 4:10-18 - Moses
Exodus 20:3-17 - The Decalogue
Numbers 12:1-15 - Aaron and Miriam
Numbers 21:4-9 - The Grumbling Israelites
Deuteronomy 21:18 - God's View of Rebellion
Joshua 7:1-26 - Achan
Judges 6:11-24 - Gideon
I Samuel 15:1-21 - Saul
I Samuel 24:1-15 - David
I Kings 18:21-40 - Elijah
II Kings 5:1-14 - Naaman
Proverbs 6:20-23 – Commands of Father, Teachings of Mother
Jeremiah 35:1-19 - The Rechabite Household
Daniel 4:28-37 - Nebuchadnezzar
Jonah 2:10-4:3 - Jonah
Matthew 4:18-22; Luke 5:1-6 - Eager Peter
Matthew 7:21-27 - Houses on Two Foundations
Matthew 9:9 - Matthew the Tax Collector
Matthew 13:1-9; 13:18-22 - Different Responses to the Word
Matthew 26:36-45 - Jesus' Agony
Mark 9:31-33; John 13:1-9; 18:1-11 - Presumptuous Peter
Luke 2:52 - Jesus, An obedient son
Luke 9:57-62 - Would-be Follower
Luke 19:1-10 - Zacchaeus
Ephesians 6:1 - Children, Obey Your Parents
Colossians 3:20 - Children, Obey Your Parents

2 Chronicles 31:21 - In everything that he undertook in the service of God's temple and in **obedience to the law and the commands**, he sought his God and worked wholeheartedly. And so he prospered.

Proverbs 6:20-23 – My son, keep your father's commands and do not forsake your mother's teaching. Bind them upon your heart forever, fasten them around your neck. When you walk, they will guide you, when you sleep, they will watch over you; when you awake, they will speak to you. For these commands are a lamp, this teaching is a light, and the corrections of **discipline** are the way to life..

Romans 5:19 - For just as through the disobedience of the one man the many were made sinners, so **also through the obedience of the one man** the many will be made righteous.

Romans 6:16 - Don't you know that when you offer yourselves to someone to obey him as slaves, you are slaves to the one whom you obey--whether you are slaves to sin, which leads to death, or to **obedience, which leads to righteousness?**

2 Corinthians 10:6 - And we will be ready to punish every act of disobedience, once your **obedience is complete**.

Hebrews 5:8 - Although he was a son, he **learned obedience** from what he suffered

2 John 1:6 - And this is love: **that we walk in obedience to his commands**. As you have heard from the beginning, his command is that you walk in love.

2 Corinthians 10:5 - We demolish arguments and every pretension that sets itself up against the knowledge of God, and we take captive **every thought to make it obedient to Christ.**

James 3:17 - But the wisdom that comes from heaven is first of all pure; then peace-loving, considerate, **submissive**, full of mercy and good fruit, impartial and sincere.

1 Peter 5:5 - **Young men, in the same way be submissive** to those who are older. All of you, clothe yourselves with humility toward one another, because, "God opposes the proud but gives grace to the humble."

Romans 13:1 - **Everyone must submit himself to the governing authorities**, for there is no authority except that which God has established. **The authorities that exist have been established by God.**

Romans 13:5 - Therefore, it is necessary to **submit to the authorities**, not only because of possible punishment but also because of conscience.

Ephesians 5:21 - **Submit to one another** out of reverence for Christ.

Hebrews 13:17 - Obey your leaders and **submit to their authority**. They keep watch over you as men who must give an account. Obey them so that their work will be a joy, not a burden, for that would be of no advantage to you.

James 4:7 - **Submit yourselves**, then, to God. Resist the devil, and he will flee from you.

1 Peter 2:13 - **Submit yourselves** for the Lord's sake to every authority instituted among men: whether to the king, as the supreme authority.

Projects and Activities

1. *Obedience* - Do a weekly evaluation of Obedience to the Ten Commandments, using a chart or jar of jelly beans to track the Obedience.

2. *Obedience/Attentiveness* - Give special rewards for the child *caught* the most times obeying without delay.

3. *Obedience* - Make a visual for the room, such as a race track, to show children's' progress on such areas as the reading of Scriptures. Charts with happy faces will give positive reinforcement to the right actions.

4. *Obedience* – Discuss how learning to obey one's parents prepares the child to obey God. Fill a jar or pocket with pebbles, small candy, or a raw bean each time a child obeys instantly.

5. *Obedience* - Make a chart for personal and household chores so children can keep track of their fulfillment of responsibilities.

6. *Obedience/Submission* - Use drama to bring home the lesson of Obedience (or disobedience) in the lives of: Abraham and Isaac; Samuel as a child; Miriam's disobedience; Mary, the mother of Jesus; Joseph; Moses suffering with his people.

7. *Obedience/Attentiveness* - Have children act out good behavior: e.g., the parent calls a child home from play, but the child disregards the call. Ask: "What would have happened if he had obeyed?" "What resulted because of his Obedience?" Act out and discuss the alternatives.

8. *Attentiveness* -Teach children to hear God's voice. See the book, *Is That Really You, God?* by Loren Cunningham, from YWAM Publishing. (See Resources)

9. Many missionary stories demonstrate Obedience to God. See the book, *Around the World*, from YWAM Publishers (See Resources)

10. *Obedience* - Invite into your home those who have obeyed or disobeyed God. The parent can interview the person. The disobedience can be put into perspective by the visitor sharing the consequences of his actions (time spent in jail, etc.).

11. *Obedience* - Research your family history and discover the outcome of Obedience or disobedience to God, in each situation. Compare the descendants of our Founding Fathers to famous criminals (Especially John

Jay; John Adams; Thomas Jefferson.) Refer to the writings of Peter Marshall Jr. (See Resources)

12. *Submission* - Study the authority Jesus demonstrated and taught His disciples. Then study our authority through Jesus over the same things. Finally, discuss the principal of Delegated Authority.

13. *Cooperativeness* - Specific needs in the child can be identified in dad-mom conferences, parent-teacher conferences, and church worker-parent conferences. Through discussion find ways the home and church or school can work together on the problem. Set goals and methods together. One son learned the importance of neatness by the teacher agreeing to place an extra mark on each paper, e.g., E/95 (excellent effort in neatness over 95% correct answers). The parent noted the extra mark and reinforced the improvement through rewards at home.

14. ✝ Discuss math facts as: always the same, and God's laws as always the same. 4+4=8; obedience=happiness; sin=unhappiness (though it may bring temporary happiness, too).

15. *Obedience* - When a child disobeys, ask him to give the definition of Obedience.

16. *Obedience* - Have older students examine what would have happened if great men of the Bible had not been Obedient. Create stories showing them in disobedience.

17. ✝ Study law and order by visiting a courtroom trial. Afterwards examine: "Why are we asked to be put under the law of our government? What would our society be like without Obedience?"

18. ✝ *One teacher arranged for a policeman to stand outside the school and give out citations on the children's bikes and other laws. Then he came into the classroom and talked about the law and Obedience.

19. ✝ Have a doctor, nurse, or dentist talk to children about consequences of not obeying the rules of hygiene.

20. ✝ Make a collage of The Ten Commandments or Psalm 19 and display it.

21. *Meekness* - Study the life of Moses: his Obedience and its results, his disobedience and its results. Do the same type study of the Israelites.

22. *Attentiveness* - Make a notebook on types of authorities and how the child will relate to each. Study God as the supreme authority, parents, teachers, etc. as delegated authority. Discuss spiritual authority.

23. *Attentiveness* - *Play a game during class or learning time to see how attentive the children can be. A sticky note for tallies can be placed at each child's place. As the lesson is proceeding, casually mark the tallies for signs of attentiveness. Collect them for the day or the week, and let them choose a reward.

24. *Cooperativeness* - Find a neighborhood project or family project for practicing cooperation. Plant and nurture a garden, or do yard work for an elderly person, or clean up an empty lot, or create a new game complete with game board and rules, or design play money and products to sell.

25. *Attentiveness* -Teach young and older children alike the simple hand signals or codes for behavior in public places. Example 1: in a group, the leader holds up 1, then after about ten seconds, 2 fingers. As any child notices the finger being help up, he mimics it. As others notice, they also use the signal. By three fingers, the entire group should be silent and watching the leader for further instruction. Example 2: Children in public settings learn to be alert and obedient without spoken words by watching their parent/s for coded signals for behavior, instructions, and correction. This can be a wink, a tap on the shoulder, etc.

26. ✝ Using Bible Facts in Psalm 19:10, 11, study the gold refining process or the making of honey to understand the way God purifies us so that we can be useful for His purposes.

27. ✝ Do a word study on these words from Psalm 19: law; statutes; precepts; commands; ordinances.

28. ✝ Study the orderliness of our own solar system and the laws of nature.

Reminder: There are general suggestions for Projects and Activities listed on Page 125 that may apply to this Unit Study.

Responsibility

Key Verse

RESPONSIBILITY – We constantly pray for you, that our God may count you worthy of his calling, and that by his power he may fulfill every good purpose of yours and every act prompted by your faith.
2 Thessalonians 1:11

CAUTIOUSNESS - Only be careful, and watch yourselves closely so that you do not forget the things your eyes have seen or let them slip from your heart as long as you live. Teach them to your children and to their children after them.
Deuteronomy 4:9

DECISIVENESS - If any of you lacks wisdom, he should ask God, who gives generously to all without finding fault, and it will be given to him. James 1:5

DILIGENCE - Whatever you do, work at it with all your heart, as working for the Lord, not for men.
Colossians 3:23

INITIATIVE - Do not be overcome by evil, but overcome evil with good.
Romans 12:21

ORDERLINESS - Everything should be done in a fitting and orderly way.
1 Corinthians 14:40

Definitions

RESPONSIBILITY is learning and following through with what God and those in charge of me expect.

CAUTIOUSNESS is knowing how important right timing and choices are in accomplishing right actions. *Wary, watchful, careful to avoid evils; attentive to examine probable effects and consequences; prudence with regard to danger.*

DECISIVENESS is devoting all my energy to a course of action which I know is right. *Conclusive, putting an end to controversy.*

DILIGENCE – is working hard at each task I am given, as though it were a special assignment from the Lord. *Constant effort to accomplish what is undertaken; care; heed (Webster quotes Proverbs 4:23.)*

INITIATIVE is seeing a need and doing something about it without being told.

ORDERLINESS is having everything in its place; organizing and utilizing my resources to their greatest efficiency. *A state of being methodical.*

PUNCTUALITY - There is a time for everything. Ecclesiastes 3:1

PUNCTUALITY is showing high esteem for other people and their time by not keeping them waiting. *Done at the exact time.*

RESOURCEFULNESS - Whoever can be trusted with very little can also be trusted with much, and whoever is dishonest with very little will also be dishonest with much. Luke 16:10

RESOURCEFULNESS is doing better work by finding new ways to use my time and material.

THOROUGHNESS - The heart of the discerning acquires knowledge; the ears of the wise seek it out. Proverbs 18:15

THOROUGHNESS is completing the details I do not like on a task as carefully as the parts I enjoy.

THRIFTINESS - So if you have not been trustworthy in handling worldly wealth, who will trust you with true riches? Luke 16:11

THRIFTINESS is making careful use of money and items at my disposal. *Economic management.*

Hymn

Give of Your Best to the Master

Give of your best to the Master;
Give of the strength of your youth;
Throw your soul's fresh glowing ardor
Into the battle for truth.
Jesus has set the example;
Dauntless was He, young and brave;
Give Him your loyal devotion,
Give Him the best that you have.

Give of your best to the Master
Give Him first place in your heart
Give Him first place in your service,
Consecrate ev'ry part.
Give, and to you shall be given;
God His beloved Son gave;
Gratefully seeking to serve Him,
Give Him the best that you have.

Give of your best to the Master;
Naught else is worthy His love;
He gave Himself for your ransom,
Gave up His glory above;
Laid down His life without murmur,
You from sin's ruin to save;
Give Him your heart's adoration,
Give Him the best that you have.

Scripture for Memorization and Meditation

Romans 12:3, 6-8

12:3 - For by the grace given me I say to every one of you: Do not think of yourself more highly than you ought, but rather think of yourself with sober judgment, in accordance with the measure of faith God has given you.

12:6 - We have different gifts, according to the grace given us. If a man's gift is prophesying, let him use it in proportion to his faith.

12:7 - If it is serving, let him serve; if it is teaching, let him teach;

12:8 - if it is encouraging, let him encourage; if it is contributing to the needs of others, let him give generously; if it is leadership, let him govern diligently; if it is showing mercy, let him do it cheerfully.

Bible Passages for Study

Genesis 39:7-20 – Joseph
Exodus 16:4 – Gathering Manna
Ruth 3:6-13 – Boaz
2 Samuel 11:8-13 - Uriah
Nehemiah 8:18 – Reading the Word
Psalm 61:8 – Fulfilling Vows
Psalm 88:9 – Prayer
Proverbs 8:34 – Watchfulness
Matthew 10:8 – Ministering According to One's Gift
Mathew 25:35 – Looking After the Needy
Luke 9:23 – Bearing One's Cross
Luke 19:13 – Seizing Opportunities
Hebrews 3:13 – Exhorting One Another
1 Peter 4:10 – Stewardship
Proverbs 4:23 – Guarding One's Heart

Proverbs 10:4 - Lazy hands make a man poor, but diligent hands bring wealth.
Proverbs 12:24 - Diligent hands will rule, but laziness ends in slave labor.
Proverbs 12:27 - The lazy man does not roast his game, but the diligent man prizes his possessions.
Proverbs 13:4 - The sluggard craves and gets nothing, but the desires of the diligent are fully satisfied.
1 Timothy 4:15 - Be diligent in these matters; give yourself wholly to them, so that everyone may see your progress.
2 Corinthians 8:17 - For Titus not only welcomed our appeal, but he is coming to you with much enthusiasm and on his own initiative.

Projects and Activities

1. *Thriftiness* - Find new uses for things you already have rather than discarding them. I.e. save small items to use in craft or art projects: water bottle caps, film canisters, tissue and paper towel cardboards, small stones, straws, breath mint tins, etc. Talk about the way our ancestors and even much of the rest of the world, makes use of every item.

2. *Thriftiness* - Provide each child with a heavy piece of cardboard and glue, using some of the things saved from #1, to create crafts from odds and ends, such as paper towels, camera film containers, cloth, chips of wood, pieces of ribbon, etc.

3. *Thriftiness* - Start a compost pile for fertilizer in your yard or garden. Discuss how this makes positive use of food waste instead of feeding the sewage plant.

4. *Responsibility* - Teach responsibility through use of contracts. These agreements between two or more parties can come out of group discussions, and can be entered into with oversight from an adult. There must be a consequence in case the contract is broken. They need to be tested before, after, and perhaps at three-month intervals. For example: one contract on an individual level concerned a boy who was careless with his belongings and the neatness of his schoolwork. The boy agreed to put each of his belongings in the locations he selected with the understanding that if his parents found anything in the wrong place, the boy would have to do a certain chore of his choosing. The boy never did have to do that chore.

5. *Cautiousness* - Play games that can illustrate the concept of cautiousness. Examples: Don't Spill the Beans; Jenga; Kerplunk; Operation; and Checkers.

6. *Diligence/Thoroughness* - With young children, use a *Happy Home Award* to teach consistency. Two weeks maximum on areas such as: brushing teeth, making beds, setting table, etc. Reward should be immediate upon completion of the time period.

7. *Initiative* - This is a good Unit Study to train parents toward giving encouraging words, comments, pats on the back, and other positive feed back methods and habits. It is easy and tempting to give negative feedback, which can lead to discouragement.

8. *Thoroughness* - Do an art project using "pointalism" (making an entire picture out of tiny dots). This requires attention to detail, concentration, and thoroughness.

9. *Punctuality* - By having fire or evacuation drills and using a stop watch, you can practice punctuality. Each person has his/her responsibility to retrieve certain items and exit the house to a predetermined meeting place. Repeat the drill trying to improve the time.

10. *Punctuality* - Discuss the importance of punctuality and how being late is stealing other people's time while they wait for the late person.

11. *Punctuality* - To teach children the concept of time: interrupt an activity and tell them they have five minutes to finish the activity. Two minutes later tell them they have three minutes left. One minute before, remind them again. When this is done frequently, most children learn to subconsciously estimate the time it take to do things. This means the adult needs to be honest about the remaining time – true to the clock.

12. *Orderliness* - To teach neatness, provide each child with his own clothes hamper or basket. Much timeless wisdom can be found in the writings of men and women of our nation's early history. Make him responsible for placing all his dirty clothes in it by himself. Give praise for even the smallest effort. Older children can learn to do their own laundry and ironing.

13. *Responsibility* - Study the biography of a person from history who showed one of the Sub-Qualities. Many of America's founding fathers were habitual journal keepers and note takers. Ben Franklin collected words of wisdom about living life responsibly and orderly. George Washington wrote lists of conduct for young men.

14. *Diligence/Thoroughness* - Tackle a household job that will take considerable time. Employ the children as if it were a job outside the home. Give them job descriptions, wages, work hours, etc. This is excellent training for their future. Remember to discuss the results. Don't forget to discuss attitudes.

15. *Diligence/Thoroughness/Responsibility/Neatness/Thriftiness* - Have a family yard sale. Determine together how the proceeds will be used: church, missions project; family trip, etc. Have each child go through his belongings and make three piles: keep, sell, throw away. Clean and polish or repair the items. Price things as a family; display them nicely; advertise; all old enough can help staff and serve as money keeper.

16. *Responsibility/Orderliness/Punctuality/Neatness* - A new pet acquired during this Unit Study would be a wonderful tool to teach the principles of: responsibility; orderliness, punctuality, neatness.

17. Devote a weekend to a big project such as cleaning the garage, working on Grandma's yard, etc. Focus on thoroughness, orderliness, diligence, and adopting a positive attitude. Follow up with a fun family outing.

18. Spend an entire dinner hour trying to anticipate each other's wishes and needs: setting the table; cutting vegetables; getting ice; passing food; refilling drinks. Discuss afterwards how initiative blesses others.

19. *Thoroughness* - Do some deep cleaning as a family. Choose appropriate things for each child to do that normally get neglected. Discuss how diligence is required to keep a house from getting dirty.

20. *Orderliness* - Have each person organize his own closet and drawers.

21. *Orderliness* - After the preceding project, have a contest to see which child can keep his or her closet and drawers neatest for one month.

22. *Responsibility* - Have each small child follow one simple instruction and then come back and get a hug. Example: "Open the window." Next, give two instructions. Example: "Put the cat outside and turn off the bathroom light. Then come back and get a hug." This teaches young children both how to follow compound instructions and responsibility, thoroughness, and diligence.

23. *Decisiveness/Diligence* - Make a game of testing concentration by doing a task while another person tries to distract. Example: playing the piano, or whistling a song while another is singing a different song in the whistler's ear; counting by threes when someone else is counting by twos.

Reminder: There are general suggestions for Projects and Activities listed on Page 125 that may apply to this study.

Virtue

Key Verse

VIRTUE – The goal of this command is love, which comes from a pure heart and a good conscience and a sincere faith. 1Timothy 1:5

CONSIDERATION – Do nothing out of selfish ambition or vain conceit, but in humility consider others better than yourself. Each of you should look not only to your own interests, but also to the interests of others. Philippians 2:3, 4

GENEROSITY – Remember this: Whoever sows sparingly will also reap sparingly, and whoever sows generously will also reap generously. 2 Corinthians 9:6

GOODNESS – Let your light shine before men that they may see your good deeds, and praise your Father in heaven. Matthew 5:16

HELPFULNESS – Anyone, then, who knows the good he ought to do and doesn't do it, sins. James 4:17

KINDNESS – Love is patient, love is kind, …it is not rude, it is not self-seeking. 1 Corinthians 13:4, 5

Definitions

VIRTUE is doing right with such joy that I help my family and friends want to do right also.

CONSIDERATION is putting another person's needs or comfort before my own. *Given to sober reflection; thoughtful; careful; discreet; not hasty or rash; not negligent.*

GENEROSITY is realizing that all I have belongs to God, and using it for His purposes.

GOODNESS is being on the inside the way I want others to see me on the outside. *Valid; sound; perfect in its kind; conformable to the moral law.*

HELPFULNESS is looking for ways to make things easier or better for others. *Assistance; usefulness.*

KINDNESS is using gentle words and thoughtful deeds to show how important each person is to God. *Cheerfully contributing to the happiness of others.*

PEACEMAKING – Peacemakers who sow in peace raise a harvest of righteousness. James 3:18

PEACEMAKING is using my time and efforts to restore broken friendships. *One who makes peace by reconciling parties that are at variance.*

PURITY – Since we have these promises, dear friends, let us purify ourselves from everything that contaminates body and spirit, perfecting holiness out of reverence for God. 2 Corinthians 7:1

PURITY is loving God by living a life free of improper views and actions – keeping a clean conscience.

SELF-CONTR0L – Those who belong to Christ Jesus have crucified the sinful nature with its passions and desires. Since we live by the Spirit, let us keep in step with the Spirit. Galatians 5:24, 25

SELF-CONTR0L is bringing thoughts, words, and actions under the control of the Holy Spirit. *Instant obedience to the initial promptings of God's Spirit.*

SENSITIVITY – Rejoice with those who rejoice; mourn with those who mourn. Romans 12:15

SENSITIVITY is having the ability to imagine the way another feels and acting accordingly. *Having a sense or feeling.*

SINCERITY – Now that you have purified yourselves by obeying the truth so that you have sincere love for the brothers, love one another deeply, from the heart. 1 Peter 1:22.

SINCERITY is being eager to do right with no hidden motives. *Honesty of mind or intention.*

Hymn

Fairest Lord Jesus

Fairest Lord Jesus! Ruler of all nature!
O Thou of God and man the Son!
Thee will I cherish, Thee will I honor,
Thou my soul's Glory, Joy, and Crown!

Fair are the meadows, fairer still the woodlands,
Robed in the blooming garb of spring;
Jesus is fairer, Jesus is purer,
Who makes the woeful heart to sing.

Fair is the sunshine, fairer still the moonlight,
And all the twinkling starry host:
Jesus shines brighter, Jesus shines purer
Than all the angels heav'n can boast.

Beautiful Savior! Lord of all nations!
Son of God and Son of Man!
Glory and honor, praise, adoration
Now and forevermore be Thine!

Scripture for Memorization and Meditation

Matthew 5:1-16

1-2 - Now when he saw the crowds, he went up on a mountainside and sat down. His disciples came to him, and he began to teach them, saying:

3 - Blessed are the poor in spirit, for theirs is the kingdom of heaven.

4 - Blessed are those who mourn, for they will be comforted.

5 - Blessed are the meek, for they will inherit the earth.

6 - Blessed are those who hunger and thirst for righteousness, for they will be filled.

7 - Blessed are the merciful, for they will be shown mercy.

8 - Blessed are the pure in heart, for they will see God.

9 - Blessed are the peacemakers, for they will be called sons of God.

10 - Blessed are those who are persecuted because of righteousness, for theirs is the kingdom of heaven.

11 - Blessed are you when people insult you, persecute you and falsely say all kinds of evil against you because of me.

12 - Rejoice and be glad, because great is your reward in heaven, for in the same way they persecuted the prophets who were before you.

13-14 - You are the salt of the earth. But if the salt loses its saltiness, how can it be made salty again? It is no longer good for anything, except to be thrown out and trampled by men. You are the light of the world. A city on a hill cannot be hidden.

15 - Neither do people light a lamp and put it under a bowl. Instead they put it on its stand, and it gives light to everyone in the house.

16 - In the same way, let your light shine before men, that they may see your good deeds and praise your Father in heaven.

Bible Facts

The Christians Virtues

1. **What are the Christian Virtues?** *"Make every effort to add to your faith goodness; and to goodness knowledge; and to knowledge self-control; and to self-control perseverance; and to perseverance godliness; and to godliness brotherly kindness; and to brotherly kindness love."*

2. **Where are the Christian Virtues listed?** The Second Book of Peter, Chapter 1, verses five and six.

3. **What are we told will happen if we have these Christian Virtues in increasing measure?** Verse eight tells us they will keep us from being ineffective and unproductive in our knowledge of our Lord Jesus Christ.

4. **What will we be like without them?** Verse nine tells us that if anyone does not have them, he is nearsighted and blind, and has forgotten that he has been cleansed from his past sins.

Bible Passages for Study

Genesis 37-42 – The Life of Joseph
Judges 13-16 – Examples, mostly negative, from Samson's life
Note: Samson lacked Virtue even though God used him mightily.
1 Samuel 15:10-35 Samuel
1 Samuel 25 – Abigail
2 Samuel 12:1-14 – Nathan
1 Kings 18:17-40; 21:17-24 – Elijah
Nehemiah 5:1-13; 13:1-31 – Nehemiah and the Jews
Psalm 19:13 – Prayer for purity
Psalm 24:3,4 – Purity before the Lord
Many Proverbs, especially in Chapters 2, 6, 7, 15, 16, and 23
Proverbs 31:10-31 – God's Ideal Woman
Daniel 1-6 – Daniel
Matthew 3:7-12; 14:1-11 – John the Baptist
Matthew 25:14-30 – The Rich Man
Luke 10:30-37 – The Good Samaritan

Colossians 3:14 - And over all **these virtues** put on love, which binds them all together in perfect unity.

Titus 3:2 - to slander no one, to be **peaceable** and **considerate**, and to show true humility toward all men.

1 Peter 3:7 - Husbands, in the same way be **considerate** as you live with your wives, and treat them with respect as the weaker partner and as heirs with you of the gracious gift of life, so that nothing will hinder your prayers.

Psalm 112:5 - Good will come to him who is **generous** and lends freely, who conducts his affairs with justice.

Proverbs 11:25 - A **generous** man will prosper; he who refreshes others will himself be refreshed.

Proverbs 22:9 - A **generous** man will himself be blessed, for he shares his food with the poor.

Galatians 5:22 - But the fruit of the Spirit is love, joy, peace, patience, **kindness**, **goodness**, faithfulness.

Ephesians 4:29 - Do not let any unwholesome talk come out of your mouths, but only what is helpful for building others up according to their needs, that it may benefit those who listen.

Proverbs 12:25 - An anxious heart weighs a man down, but a **kind** word cheers him up.

Proverbs 14:21- He who despises his neighbor sins, but blessed is he who is **kind** to the needy.

Proverbs 19:17 - He who is **kind** to the poor lends to the LORD, and he will reward him for what he has done.

2 Timothy 2:24 - And the Lord's servant must not quarrel; instead, he must be **kind** to everyone, able to teach, not resentful.

1 Thessalonians 5:15 - Make sure that nobody pays back wrong for wrong, but always try to be **kind** to each other and to everyone else.

Matthew 5:9 - Blessed are the **peacemakers**, for they will be called sons of God.

James 3:18 **- Peacemakers** who sow in peace raise a harvest of righteousness.

Proverbs 22:11 - He who loves a **pure** heart and whose speech is gracious will have the king for his friend.

Proverbs 25:28 - Like a city whose walls are broken down is a man who lacks self-control.

Galatians 5:23 - ......gentleness and **self-control**. Against such things there is no law.

Romans 12:9 - Love must be **sincere**. Hate what is evil; cling to what is **good**.

James 3:17 - But the wisdom that comes from heaven is first of all **pure**; then **peace-loving**, **considerate**, submissive, full of mercy and **good** fruit, impartial and sincere.

Proverbs 12:22 - The LORD detests lying lips, but he delights in men who are truthful.

Proverbs 14:25 - A truthful witness saves lives, but a false witness is deceitful.

Projects and Activities

1. ✝ Do a word study on the word *fair* as in the Hymn, *Fairest Lord Jesus*.

2. *Goodness* - Discuss the fallacy in the fairy tale of "Snow White" where the woman says, "Mirror, mirror on the wall, who's the fairest of them all?" Use the definition of the word *goodness*.

3. *Goodness* - Rewrite portions of the Snow White story with the understanding of purity demonstrating true beauty and goodness.

4. *Goodness/Kindness* - Do a synonym search for the words: *kind*, *nice*, and *good*. Have a writing assignment using the words found.

5. *Virtue* - Although it is difficult to pinpoint Virtue, we need to see it in our peers. To help children identify Goodness and Kindness in family members, relatives, and friends, make "I was caught being Good/Kind" badges or stickers. Have a week where each time a family member sees an act of Kindness in another, he says, "I caught you being Kind…" (explaining how). Then that person wears a badge or sticker for the rest of the day.

6. *Virtue* - Study the Kings of Israel and Judah in the Old Testament. Discuss which kings displayed Virtue; how; and why. Which ones displayed immorality; how.

7. ✝ Older students can illustrate the Sermon on the Mount; younger children can make an illustrated book from pictures using a copier, printer, scanner, or magazines, showing goodness.

8. *Goodness* - Have children commend another child in the group, naming Character Qualities. Instruct them to describe how the Character Quality was expressed, rather than to use the word *nice*.

9. *Generosity* - Create a story using the concepts from Jesus' mention of the Widow's Mite in Mark 12:41 - 44. Encourage the children to include: Who was she? What were the reasons for her circumstances? What caused her to give her last pennies? Fictionalize missing facts.

11. *Purity* - Study how precious metals are purified and discuss the application to ourselves. See Zechariah 13:9; Malachi 3:3.

12. *Kindness* – Have an older child take on "kindness in action" toward a person they see regularly, but who is treated by others as a misfit.

13. *Helpfulness/ Consideration* – Develop new habits of helpfulness and consideration by spending 21 days finding ways to practice them.

14. *Peacemaking* - Discuss how conflict in one's life is about a root problem, not only the surface demonstration or circumstance at hand. Find ways to look deeper into conflicts and fix the root problems.

15. *Peacemaking* - Stage a debate about something that is negotiable. Have one child serve as arbiter and the others present their case/s. Someone can debate from a side of the issue that he/she doesn't agree with. The exercise is to teach the arbiter or mediator how to be a peacemaker through compromise or calm discussion.

16. *Peacemaker* - Agree that each person will look for examples of conflict. Observe them at stores, at home, in the car next to you, etc. After a few days, discuss what each has witnessed and how the concepts of this Unit were or could have been applied.

17. *Generosity* - Study the difference between tithing and free will offerings as found in both the Old and New Testaments. Have each student explain how generosity is shown in these scriptures, and how we might apply examples today.

18. *Generosity* - Study the life of a missionary or philanthropist. Explore how the person gave all they had to serve others and how their life was affected by their generosity. How other people's lives were affected by it.

19. *Self-Control* - Read together the book, *Whatever Happened to Justice?,* from the Uncle Eric Series, by Richard Maybury, Bluestocking Press. (See Resources) Notice and discuss "The Two Fundamental Laws."

20. *Self-Control* - Explore the idea of The Golden Rule and how to discipline one's self with controlled behavior.

21. *Generosity/Kindness/Sensitivity* - Sponsor a needy child or family, or even an individual. Write or visit the person and develop an on-going relationship with him. Write letters that include notes from each family member. Learn how you can meet specific needs. Put their picture on the refrigerator and pray regularly as a family for him.

22. *Virtue* – Gather a collection of scenes and faces from famous artists from the Renaissance forward. Find a face or scene for each of this Unit's Qualities. Write a caption or description for each, or use them as a springboard for creative writing.

Love – God's Grace

Note: God's Love, His Grace, and Mercy are not typical Character studies. They are more *Truth* and *Principles*, than they are Character Qualities. As we learn what Jesus did for us in the plan of salvation, we also need to understand that we will be required to apply these truths to our own behavior toward those around us, especially when we feel they do not deserve it.

Key Verse	Definition
GOD'S LOVE – For God so loved the world that he gave his one and only son, that whoever believes in him shall not perish but have eternal life. John 3:16	**LOVE** is choosing to look at another through God's eyes as one of worth, value, and potential.
GRACE – For it is by grace you have been saved, through faith—and this not from yourselves, it is the gift of God—not by works, so that no one can boast. Ephesians 2:8,9	**GRACE** is the willingness to treat another as though he has no faults or sins.
MERCY – Learn what this means: I desire mercy, not sacrifice. For I have not come to call the righteous, but sinners. Matthew 9:13	**MERCY** is the willingness to withhold judgment or punishment that another deserves.

Hymn

I Love to Tell the Story

I love to tell the story of unseen things above,
Of Jesus and His glory, of Jesus and His love.
I love to tell the story, because I know 'tis true;
It satisfies my longing as nothing else can do.

I love to tell the story; more wonderful it seems
Than all the golden fancies of all our golden dreams.
I love to tell the story, it did so much for me;
And that is just the reason I tell it now to thee.

I love to tell the story; 'tis pleasant to repeat
What seems each time I tell it more wonderfully sweet.
I love to tell the story, for some have never heard
The message of salvation from God's own holy Word.

I love to tell the story, for those who know it best
Seem hungering and thirsting to hear it like the rest.
And when, in scenes of glory, I sing the new, new song,
'Twill be the old, old story, that I have loved so long.

~ Chorus ~

I love to tell the story, 'twill be my theme in glory,
To tell the old, old story of Jesus and His love.

Scripture for Memorization and Meditation

Romans 8:28

28 - And we know that in all things God works for the good of those who love him, who have been called according to his purpose.

29 - For those God foreknew he also predestined to be conformed to the likeness of his Son, that he might be the firstborn among many brothers.

30 - And those he predestined, he also called; those he called, he also justified; those he justified, he also glorified.

31- What, then, shall we say in response to this? If God is for us, who can be against us?

32 - He who did not spare his own Son, but gave him up for us all--how will he not also, along with him, graciously give us all things?

33 - Who will bring any charge against those whom God has chosen? It is God who justifies.

34 - Who is he that condemns? Christ Jesus, who died--more than that, who was raised to life--is at the right hand of God and is also interceding for us.

35 - Who shall separate us from the love of Christ? Shall trouble or hardship or persecution or famine or nakedness or danger or sword?

36 - As it is written: "For your sake we face death all day long; we are considered as sheep to be slaughtered."

37 - No, in all these things we are more than conquerors through him who loved us.

38 - For I am convinced that neither death nor life, neither angels nor demons, neither the present nor the future, nor any powers,

39 - Neither height nor depth, nor anything else in all creation, will be able to separate us from the love of God that is in Christ Jesus our Lord.

Bible Facts

The Gospel

1. **What does the word G*ospel* mean?** Gospel means good news.

2. **What is the Good News in the Bible?** The good news is the wonderful story of Christ's death and resurrection which brings salvation.

3. **How does a Christian feel about the Good News?** Romans 1:16 tells us that a Christian is proud to talk about the Good News because it brings salvation to everyone who believes.

4. **Why does everyone need salvation?** Romans 3:23 tells us that everyone has sinned.

5. **How did God show His love for sinners?** Romans 5:8 tells us that Christ died for us while we were sinners, showing God's love for us.

6. **Can salvation be earned or purchased?** No. Romans 6:23 tells us that salvation is a gift of God.

7. **Is God's gift given to us only to bring us to heaven**? No. Romans 8:28 tells us that God is working all things together for our highest good in this life.

8. **How does a person receive God's gift?** Romans 10:9 tells us to believe in Jesus' resurrection in our hearts and to confess Him as Lord with our mouths.

9. **Who may receive God's gift?** Romans 10:13 tells us that anyone who calls on the Lord's name will be saved.

10. **How should a Christian behave when he sees and understands God's great love**? Romans 12:1 tells us that we should give our whole life to God as a sacrifice that pleases Him.

11. **Name in order the eight verses that tell the Good News about Jesus Christ.** Romans 1:16; 3:23; 5:8; 6:23; 8:28; 10:9; 10:13; 12:1

Bible Passages for Study

The Romans Road

Romans 1:14-17 – The Gospel is Good News
Romans 3:9-20 – But First, the Bad News
Romans 3:21-26 – Jesus Came Just in Time
Romans 6:15-23 – Sin Pays Death; God Gives Life
Romans 8:28-39 – A Happy Life, Not Just an Unending One
Romans 10:9, 10, 13 – He's Just a Call Away
Romans 12:1,2 – All He Wants is You

The Book of Ruth – Example of God's Grace to Ruth
The Book of Jonah – Example of God's Forgiveness
Matthew 18:21-35 – Story of the Unjust Steward
Letter to Philemon – Philemon is Asked to Extend Love, Grace, and Mercy to His Run-away Slave, Onesimus.
1 Samuel – David's Attitude and Treatment of Saul
Acts 11:25 – Barnabas' Acceptance of Saul/Paul
Acts 15:36 – Compare with the above passage
Ephesians 2:3b-10 –We've Been Given a Gift of Worth

Projects and Activities

1. Research and write a Thank You Prayer with Jesus' picture on the front showing the horror of the 39 stripes, the crucifixion, etc.

2. Read the book *Shepherd of the Hills* and discuss how **Love**, **Grace**, and **Mercy** are expressed.

3. Rent the movie: *The Passion of the Christ*, for older children to watch. Have them watch for the underlying teachings of God's Love and Forgiveness.

4. Read the books: *The Hiding Place* and *Peace Child*. Discuss *forgiveness* and *peace* through ultimate sacrifice of love, etc.

5. Read and discuss the story, *Gift of the Magi*.

6. Take a close look at Europe's most famous fairy tales: Snow White; Cinderella; Sleeping Beauty, etc. and notice the correlation between the hero and the Prince of Peace, and the girl and lost mankind. If you can read the oldest version in print, this is clearer than the modern Disney-type versions. In older versions, the Prince had to spill his blood or do a great feat.

7. Make a Wordless Book or a charm bracelet together. Practice telling the *story* to others. (Black represents sin; red – Christ's blood; white – salvation; green – new life, gold – heaven.)

Reminder: There are general suggestions for Projects and Activities on Page 125 that may apply to this Unit Study.

General Projects and Activities

Note: Many of these general ideas may be used with one Character Quality at a time, over and over again, until the family or class has developed their collections into categorized groupings.

1. Discuss the full meaning of the word *critique*: the art of estimating the qualities or value of art or literature. Discuss the fact that the conclusion can be negative or positive. Spend a Saturday morning watching and critiquing children's cartoons. Ask which ones demonstrate Character Qualities and topics worthy of a godly child's time. Which ones glorify negative Qualities?
2. Look through your children's fairy tales and sort or label the stories by the Positive or Negative Qualities they portray. (See list of Positive and Negative Qualities beginning on Page 11.)
3. Find a fairy tale such as *Hansel and Gretel*, or a Disney cartoon such as *The Little Mermaid*, to critique. Look at the main character's positive or negative character traits and discuss them.
4. Retell the story above in a creative writing assignment and show more godly traits being demonstrated or learned by the character.
5. Do the above with the family's video game collection, or teen's music collection, or an evening's viewing of TV shows.
6. Go through the book of Psalms or Proverbs and group the Qualities you are studying.
7. Have the children look through the family's Christian music collection and find songs that go well with the Character Quality you're studying. Create a new CD or tape with those songs.
8. Develop an exercise choreography for one or two songs. Use this as part of your Physical Education time.
9. Develop worship choreography for one or two songs. This broadens the avenues of learning and expression for the Character Quality.
10. Develop skits for appropriate songs.
11. On a cassette, record a *radio show*, or use a video camera to dramatize a Bible story or fairy tale that demonstrates the Character Quality being studied.
12. Illustrate a story using a comic book format.
13. Illustrate a story using a camera, to create a *story board* or *a still picture storybook* to follow.
14. Have older children research a virtuous Old Testament man or woman, then write a fictional story based on Bible Facts. Present the story as a monologue, dressing as that character.

15. Character Fairs have proven successful in bonding families with others by providing a common focal point. Each family, or each child, presents a Project having to do with the Character Quality being studied. Types of Projects include: slide presentations, scrap books, dramas, poems, and stories.
16. Have a family-drama-night using Bible stories or fairy tales that were written in #4 above. Dress up, use props, change your voices, and dramatize! Have someone video the fun.
17. Individuals with no obvious good Character Qualities sometimes can be subtly, slowly changed by someone noticing a hint of a godly Character Quality, commending the person for it, and noticing when the Quality appears again. Most people beam at the mention of a good Character Quality in their lives. Try this as an experiment and report the result to the others.
18. During your vocabulary and spelling lesson, use words from the list of Sub-Qualities for the Character Quality being studied. (The list is inside the front cover and with the Key Verses at the beginning of each Unit). Study synonyms, antonyms, words from the Bible stories, etc.
19. Introduce a Unit of Study by bringing up a story from your past illustrating the Character Quality and how you learned it.
20. Interview grandparents if they are nearby. If they live at a distance, ask them to record stories from their lives where they learned about the Character Quality being studied. (If the recording must pass through the mail, you'll need to ask them in advance of the Unit.)
21. Study, celebrate, or observe various Jewish feasts and holidays in order to discover the principles, truths, and Qualities that God was teaching through them.
22. Go through your personal library and find books, and novels that demonstrate the desired Qualities. Write these into your lesson plans instead of the school reading books.
23. Go to a Christian bookstore or library and do the above.
24. Use daily practice of penmanship to teach and reinforce self-discipline, to develop the soul, and mind, instead of simply using material that would be busy work. Include Bible verses, Quality definitions, selections of poetry, or lines from literature that reinforce the lessons you are teaching.
25. By using paper with colorable borders for the above, you can add fun and make the items something worth keeping, even frame for display.
26. *If you have a needle crafter to finish the Project, have children make squares for a quilt illustrating the verses they memorized.
25. Go through family photo albums and focus on pictures that spark stories. Guide a discussion about accomplishments of family or friends displaying the qualities.
28. Gather a collection of scenes and faces from famous artists from the Renaissance forward. Find a face or scene for each of this Unit's Qualities. Write a caption or description for each, or use them as a springboard for creative writing.

Resources

Many of these Resources can be used in more than one of the Unit Studies. Because available titles change frequently, rather than listing individual titles, beginning in this Sixth Edition, we are listing primarily suppliers.

Listing in the Handbook does not indicate endorsement of the materials. Nor does exclusion indicate a supplier may not have excellent materials. Inclusion in this list is simply to help facilitate your locating materials that will help you to develop godly character in your children. There are so many available, it is impossible for us to include all. We suggest you use the Internet, and go to some of the many "Christian supplier" and "homeschool" search engines. Type in the Character Quality you are looking for.

We suggest you contact the supplier and ask for catalogs that list their "home school" or "parenting" materials. Some may ask you to send a self-address, stamped envelope with adequate postage to cover the cost of mailing. If you don't have a Christian bookstore near you, this may be worth the cost. Unless instructed otherwise, place the postage stamps in the upper right hand corner of the 8 ½ x 11 inch envelope, address it to yourself, and put it, folded once, inside a smaller envelope address to the supplier.

Seminars and Workshops – Note that these seminars share godly principles for daily living and for understanding family relationships. They are excellent tools for a strong family foundation. However, be aware that there may be a tendency for some individuals to extend a good principle into an excuse for legalism.

Christian Life Workshops, P.O. Box 2250, Gresham OR 97030, (800) 225-5259

Institute in Basic Life Principles, IBLP Headquarters, Box One, Oak Brook, IL 60522-3001, 630-323-9800, iblp.org, info@iblp.org

Catalog Distributors:

Appalachian Distributors, PO Box 1573, 522 Princeton Road, Johnson City, TN 3760, (800) 289-2772, www.appalink.com/forms/servant.htm

Christian Book Distributors, (CBD) 140 Summit Street, P.O. Box 6000, Peabody, CA 01961-6000, (800) 247-4784, www.christianbook.com/

Individual Publishers and Suppliers:

Mantle Ministries, Richard (Little Bear) Wheeler, 228 Still Ridge Bulverde, TX 78163-1878, (830) 438-3777, orders@mantleministries.com, info@mantleministries.com, www.mantlemin.com/

The Association of Christian School International, www.acsi.org/acsi/Welcome.aspx

Augsburg Press, Augsburg Fortress, P.O. Box 1209, Minneapolis, MN 55440-1209, (800) 328-4648, www.augsburgfortress.org/contactus/

Barbour & Company, Inc., info@barbourbooks.com, www.barbourbooks.com/

Bethany House Publishers, A division of Baker Books, 11400 Hampshire Ave. S., Bloomington, MN 55438 (952) 829-2500, www.bethanyhouse.com/

Bluestocking Press, P.O. Box 2030, Shingle Springs, CA 95682-2030, 1-800-959-8586, http://www.bluestockingpress.com/

Bridgestone Multimedia (800) 622-3070 or 300 North McKemy Avenue, Chandler AZ 85226-2618, www.BridgestoneMultimedia.com

Broadman & Holman Publishers, 127 Ninth Avenue North, MSN 114, Nashville, TN. 37234, (800) 448-8032, www.broadmanholman.com/

Character Building Drama Tapes, available from Christian Education Services, Route 1, Box 71, Thonotosassa, FL 33592.

Family Restoration Seminar, a 12-tape series, taught by Gregg Harris. Available from CLW, 182 S. Kane Road, Gresham OR 97080.

Gospel Publishing House, www.gospelpublishing.com/

Peter Marshall Ministries, 81 Finlay Road, Orleans, MA 02653, (800) 879-3298, pmm@petermarshallministries.com www.petermarshallministries.com/

Christian Teaching Materials, Co. P. O. Box 639, Glenpool, OK 74033-0639 CLW, 182 S. Kane Road, Gresham OR 97080.

Concordia Publishing House, 3558 S. Jefferson, St. Louis, MO 63118-3968, (800) 325 3040, www.cph.org/

Coral Ridge Ministries, PO Box 40, Ft Lauderdale FL 33302, letters@coralridge.org, (800) 229-9673, www.coralridge.org/

Crossway Books, a division of Good News Publishers, 1300 Crescent Stl, Wheaton, IL 60187, (630) 682-4300, www.crosswaybooks.org

Cook Communications Ministries, 4050 Lee Vance View, Colorado Springs, CO 80918, (800) 708-5550 or (719) 536-0100

Family Mission/Vision Enterprises, A Division of Global Christian Network, Inc., P.O. Box 7198, Bend OR 97708-7198.
(541) 317-1763, www.cookministries.com/

Focus on the Family Magazines, from Focus on the Family, P.O. Box 35500, Colorado Springs CO 80935-3550

Gateway Films/Vision Video, 2030 Wentz Church Road, P.O. Box 540, Worcester, PA 19490-0540; (800) 523-0226 or 610-584-1893

Gazelle Publications, 11560 Berrien Springs, MI 49103. (800) 650-5076 www.hoofprints.com

Guideposts, 39 Seminary Hill Road, Carmel, NY 10512

Integrity/Hosanna Music, 1000 Cody Road, Mobile, AL 36695, (800) 533-6912 (8 a.m. -5 p.m. CST), cservice@integinc.com , (800) www.integritymusic.com/

InterVarsity Press, PO Box 1400, Downers Grove, IL 60515 , (800) 843-9487 (option 2) , customerservice@ivpress.com , (800) www.gospelcom.net/ivpress/

Josh McDowell Ministries, P.O. Box 1250, Wheaton, Ill 60189 or P.O. Box 1000C, Dallas, TX 75221

Ligonier Ministries, P.O. Box 547500, Orlando, FL 32854-7500, (800) 435-4343, www.ligonier.org/

Maranatha Music, 205 Avenida Fabricante, San Clemente CA 92672, (800) 245-7664 - press 5 (8:00am- 5:00pm PST), customerservice@corinthian.com, www.maranathamusic.com/

Memlok, Church Resource Ministries, P. O. Box 5189, Fullerton CA 92635-5189, 420 Montwood, La Habra CA 90631-7411, (800) 373-1947 PST, www.memlock.com/

Mott Media, 112 E. Ellen Street, Fenton, MI 48430-2115, (800) 421-6645 www.mottmedia.com/

Moody Publishers, 820 N. LaSalle Blvd., Chicago IL 60610, www.moodypublishers.org/

Multnomah Books, P.O. Box 1720, Sisters, OR 97759, (541)-549-1144, information@multnomahbooks.com www.multnomahbooks.com/

Navpress, P. O. Box 35002, Colorado Springs, CO 80935, (800) 366-7788, www.navpress.com/

Pearables: Character Materials, P. O. Box 9887, Colorado Springs, CO 80932, www.pearables.com/

Price/Stern/Sloan Publishers, my.linkbaton.com/bibliography/+Price+Stern+Sloan+Publishing/

Regal Books, 1957 Eastman Ave., Ventura, CA 93003 (800) 4-GOSPEL , regalbooks.com/

Shining Star Publishers, Dept. PSS91, P.O. Box 299, Carthage IL 62321-0229 (800) 435-7234

Standard Publishers, 8121 Hamilton Ave., Cincinnati, OH 45231, (513) 931-4050, customerservice@standardpub.com, (800) www.standardpub.com

Still Waters Revival Books, 4710-37A Avenue, Edmonton AB T6L 3T5 Canada, (708) 450-3730, swrb@swrb.com, www.swrb.com

The Banner of Truth Trust, PO Box 621, Carlisle, PA 17013, Tel: 717-249-5747, info@banneroftruth.org www.banneroftruth.org/pages/home.php

The Mayflower Institute, P.O. Box 4673, Thousand Oaks CA 91359, Liberty Networking Corporation, 420 North Seventh Street , Barron, WI 54812, (71) 637-0508 info@libertynetworking.com, www.libertynetworking.com, www.mayflowerinstitute.com/

The Presbyterian and Reformed Publishing Co., Philadelphia PA, 1967.

The Teaching Home Magazine, Box 20219, Portland OR 97294, (503) 253-9633, tth@teachinghome.com, www.teachinghome.com/

The Ungame, www.amazon.com

Thomas Nelson Publishers, PO Box 141000, Nashville, TN 37214, www.thomasnelson.com/

Tyndale House, 351 Executive Drive, Carol Stream, IL 60188, (800) 323-9400 www.tyndale.com/

Vineyard Music

YWAM Publishing/Emerald Books, P.O. Box 55787, Seattle, WA 98155 (800) 922-2143, customerservice@ywampublishing.com , www.ywampublishing.com/

Zondervan Publishing House, 5300 Patterson SE, Grand Rapids, MI 49530—0002, (800) 226-1122, zprod@zph.com, www.zondervan.com/

Meet the Authors and Contributors

Beverly Caruso teaches Bible classes, retreats and conferences, marriage and family seminars, plus writers' workshops and seminars. Bev and her husband Pete pastored two churches and have ministered in 40 countries. She has written several additional books and numerous articles. Bev has trained writers from twenty-five countries.

Ken Marks oversaw the development the original Christian Character Curriculum by working with the faculties while he served as the principal of Orange Christian School in Orange, California, and later, Kingwood Academy, Kingwood, Texas. In addition, he used the material as a classroom teacher. Ken is currently teaching in a public high school.

Debbie Peterson is the daughter of Bev and Pete Caruso. She was reared in a Christian School and began working as a playground supervisor while in high school, when these concepts were being introduced. Later she served as a teacher's aid and a classroom substitute teacher. Debbie home schooled her three children for thirteen years and successfully graduated all three from high school. She has spoken at numerous home school groups and conventions. Debbie is currently teaching home school children through the California public school system.

We're indebted to many for their contributions to this material - spouses and family members, parents of students, but especially to faculties and staff members of Orange Christian School and Kingwood Academy.

During the writing of the first edition of this handbook, at a gathering of teachers, former students and home school parents, all experienced with using this material, project ideas were shared. We hope their experiences will trigger Projects that will "bring home" the application of Character Qualities in your children's lives. Members of the group and their professional experience ***prior to*** the time of the gathering:

Alice Donar taught for sixteen years at third, fifth and sixth-grade levels.

Maxine Doyle taught for eighteen years at first, second and fourth grade levels.

Renee Green taught kindergarten, fourth grade and art, for a total of four years.

Joan Hartman taught second grade and junior high math and language arts for a total of six years.

Jerry Lujan taught seventh through tenth grades for a total of fourteen years.

Nancy Lujan taught second through sixth grades for a total of twelve years.

Nyla Marks taught kindergarten, first, second, third, and fourth grades and junior high for a total of thirteen years. She also served as music teacher and tutor for reading and math.

Joyce Matthews served as classroom aid, director of summer camp, librarian, remedial reading teacher and classroom teacher at the fourth, fifth and sixth grade levels for a total of eight years.

Gail Nicholson taught kindergarten, second, seventh and eighth grades for fourteen years.

***Misty Marks** and **Winton Nicholson** were elementary and junior high school students using this material for seven years.

We have been greatly influenced by Bill Gothard and his Basic Life Principles Seminars. As a result, his material has become such a part of us we may fail to give proper credit for his material. We are aware that the basic outline of Ten Basic Steps of Correction originated with Bill Gothard.

Faith Builders
from
Around the World

365 Daily Readings

Compiled by Beverly Caruso

Help your children see the many aspects of God through the lives of missionaries from over ninety nations as they serve Him in some of the toughest places to take the gospel. You'll plant in their hearts a view of the world as a whole. Reinforce their studies in geography, history, cultures, and most of all God's heart.

Here are accounts of God's faithfulness, mercy, power, and care in the lives of Christians from around the globe.

Receive a daily dose of faith as you read firsthand about the God of Abraham, Isaac, and Jacob still working in the lives of people today.

Dramatic stories of frontline faith in action. A collection of firsthand reports from missionaries serving today in far flung places.

See how God continues to guide people in His service and provide for their needs. These stories reflect the different aspects of God's character at work today in lives of people of all ages and walks of life.

$10.00

Bill Bright, Founder of Campus Crusade for Christ wrote:

"...examples of what God can do through hearts totally surrendered to Him. Their stories and devotionals will inspire others to higher levels of commitment in following our wonderful Savior."

Pastor Jack Hayford says:

"*These stories are the essence of God's abiding grace, working miraculously in the greatest laboratory of all - the human soul. Let me encourage you to be refreshed by this huge handful of 'faith stimulants' - accounts of the Word of God - Jesus Himself being 'made flesh' again by the beauty of His work in people's daily lives.*"

Loving Confrontation

by Beverly Caruso

Biblical Relationship Principles for Daily Christian Living

How the Body of Christ Can Be "Fitly Joined Together"

Christ's prayer in John 17 emphasizes the unity He expects and desires in His church. Nevertheless, the whole area of loving, honest relationships proves to be a difficult calling. The tendency is to tolerate problems in each other's lives in order to avoid the personal involvement and possible hurt of confrontation. Yet the call to unity remains.

With twenty-five years of pastoral experience, Beverly Caruso and her husband have discovered biblical and practical principles that transformed their individual lives, their marriage, and their church. As they personally found god at work in the areas of speaking the truth in love, they were able to help others come into a new freedom and openness with each other.

Through true stories you will see how Christ can work in your life through **acceptance**, **forgiveness**, **sharing**, **affirming**, as well as, **confronting one another.**

$10.00

"A lot of living has gone into this account of an ordinary church which set about to remold daily relationships on biblical principles. With humor and candor Beverly Caruso recalls the mistakes and the triumphs which have brought one congregation into a brand new dimension of Christian reality. Packed with practical guidelines for those of us wanting to apply their discoveries in our own settings.... I found myself reading every line with absorption."

From **John and Elizabeth Sherrill**, writers for the authors of *The Hiding Place, God's Smuggler,* and *The Cross and the Switchblade*, and contributing editors for Guideposts Magazine.

Order Form

Quantity

_____ *Developing Godly Character in Children* (from the authors) $20.00 ____
retails for $23.95

_____ *Faith Builders from Around the World* 10.00 ____

_____ *Loving Confrontation* 10.00____

Sub-Total _____

In CA, add 8.25% tax _____

Shipping and handling - 10% of sub-total _____

Total enclosed _____

Shipping Address:

____
Name

____
Street Address

____
P.O. Box

____
City State Zip

Make checks payable and send order to:

Abba Ministries
P.O. Box 1388
Lake Elsinore, CA 92530, USA

Phone (951) 245-4082 Fax: (951) 245-9068
Email: admin@across2u.com Website:http://across2u.com/abba.html

Character Development Lesson Plan

Major Quality of Unit Study_______________ General Goal___________________

Specific measurable behavior objectives for Group:_________________________

Child #1_____________________________Child #3____________________________

Child #2_____________________________Child #4____________________________

Week #______Dates__________________

Day #1_____

Discuss and memorize Definition & Key Verse of Major Quality________________

Discuss and assign memorization of Sub-Qualities: __________________________

and: __________________________

Introduce Scripture Memorization passage_________________________________

Assign Memorization of verses for older children_____________________________

Day #2 _____

Review Definitions and Key Verses_______ Discuss Bible Facts______________

Introduce verse #_____ of Hymn _________________________on Page _______

Sing choruses: __________________________and___________________________

Read Scripture for Memorization and Meditation together____________________

Read and discuss Bible passage___________________

Long Term Project____

Resources____

Daily Activity or Lesson____

Supplies Needed____

Ways to implement and work into school subjects__________________________

____

____

Day #3 _____

Review Definitions and Key Verses______ assign Bible Facts # _______

Sing verse #______ of Hymn ________________________________ Page______

Sing________________________________and______________________________

Check on Memorization assignments_____________________________________

Read Scripture for Memorization and Meditation together____________________

Read and discuss Bible passage/s____